It's another great book from CGP...

If you can read this, you obviously know a fair bit about English Language.
But to do well at GCSE, you'll need to be able to analyse it in a lot more detail.

Not to worry. This brilliant CGP Workbook is packed with essential practice
— from exercises that test you on the basics to realistic exam-style questions.
And of course, it's all perfectly matched to the new AQA course.

Still not convinced? We've also included worked exam papers with sample answers
for you to mark, a full set of practice papers and all the answers! If we'd thought the
kitchen sink would help you get a top grade, we'd have included that too.

CGP — still the best! ☺

Our sole aim here at CGP is to produce the highest quality books —
carefully written, immaculately presented and dangerously close to being funny.

Then we work our socks off to get them out to you
— at the cheapest possible prices.

CONTENTS

CONTENTS

Published by CGP

Editors:
Emma Bonney
Joe Brazier
Emma Crighton

With thanks to Holly Poynton and Elisabeth Quincey for the proofreading.
With thanks to Laura Jakubowski for the copyright research.

Acknowledgements:

AQA material is reproduced by permission of AQA.

With thanks to iStockphoto.com for permission to use the images on pages 2, 17, 18, 32, 60 & 91.

With thanks to Getty Images for permission to use the image on pages 63 & 74.

Extract from 'The Night' by Ray Bradbury on pages 64-65 used by permission of Abner Stein.

Article entitled 'Confessions of a Nanny' on page 78 © Guardian News & Media Ltd 2013.

*Letter written by Charlotte Brontë on page 79 from 'Charlotte Brontë and Her Circle',
by Clement K. Shorter, 1896 (pages 80-82).*

Article entitled 'What are friends for?' on page 95 © Guardian News & Media Ltd 2015.

*Every effort has been made to locate copyright holders and obtain permission to reproduce sources.
For those sources where it has been difficult to trace the copyright holder of the work, we would be grateful
for information. If any copyright holder would like us to make an amendment to the acknowledgements,
please notify us and we will gladly update the book at the next reprint. Thank you.*

ISBN: 978 1 78294 370 9
Printed by Elanders Ltd, Newcastle upon Tyne.
Clipart from Corel®

Based on the classic CGP style created by Richard Parsons.

Planning Answers

Q1 Read this exam question, then answer the questions below.

> Look in detail at lines 12-21 of the source.
> How does the writer use language to describe Uncle William?

a) Underline the phrase which tells you what part of the text to write about.

b) Which character should your answer focus on? _Uncle William_

c) Circle the word which tells you which feature of the text to write about.

Q2 Here's an exam question and a plan for an answer. Write down **three** reasons why it's a good plan.

> *"It's important for young people to participate in sport."*
>
> Write a newspaper article in which you explain your point of view on this statement.
>
> <u>Plan</u>
>
> Positive view on statement: benefits of sport e.g. learning teamwork.
> My counter-argument 1: young people are busy; may not have time.
> My counter-argument 2: can get the benefits of sport in other ways.
> Conclusion: Sport is good, but we don't all have to do it.

The lack of young people involved in sport was becoming problematic for the Olympic team.

1) ....

2) ....

3) ....

Q3 Write a brief plan for an answer to the question below.

> *"Students aged 11-16 should be given a pet to care for by their school. It would teach them valuable life skills."*
>
> Write a speech to be given to your school governors in which you argue for or against this statement.

- Some may forget about the pet
- ~~wast~~ alot Of money • up the age perimeters
- 13 - 17

Don't just stare into space — get on and planet...

You don't need to plan every answer in your English Language exams, but for the longer writing questions (question 5 in each paper) it's important. Tick the self-assessment boxes below to show how well you think you've done on this page.

 ☐   ☐   ☐

P.E.E.D.

Q1 Read the following exam answers. Tick the answers which use
the P.E.E.D. technique (Point, Example, Explain, Develop).

a) The writer uses similes to make his description of Kidston's motor racing more vivid. For example, he describes Kidston's Bentley as being "like a cheetah". This shows how powerful and fast Kidston's car was. This phrase also connects Kidston with a cheetah, suggesting that he is exciting and exotic too.

b) The writer says that the racing driver Glen Kidston was rich, glamorous and charismatic. He had an exciting career in the Royal Navy, surviving several torpedo attacks, before taking up motor sports. He won the Le Mans 24-hour race in 1930, but died in a plane crash in the Drakensberg Mountains in 1931, aged just 32.

c) The writer uses rhetorical questions to get the reader to agree with their point of view. For example, he asks "Was there a finer, more determined driver than Kidston?" The rhetorical questions lead the reader to agree with the writer's opinion that Kidston was a great driver, and make the whole text more persuasive.

☐   ☐   ☐

Q2 Read the following extract from a tourist information sheet.

West Kennet Long Barrow — The Skeleton Tomb

West Kennet Long Barrow is an ancient tomb near Avebury. Here you can become a real-life tomb explorer, and experience the thrill of having history at your fingertips. There are five fascinating chambers in the tomb, where you can explore, quest and hunt to discover the secrets of a bygone age. This is probably the best-preserved tomb of its kind in the country — a real archeological treat for all ages.

Write out an example from the text that you could use to support each point below.
Then explain why your example supports the point.

a) Point: *The writer uses direct address to form a personal link with the reader.*

Example: "Having history at your finger tips"

Explanation: The writer is using your to make us think its personally for us

b) Point: *The writer also uses a combination of descriptive verbs to create a sense of adventure.*

Example: ....

Explanation: ....

....

P.E.E.D.

Q3 Read the following extract from the opening to a short story, and answer the questions below.

> Alice stepped from the bus and was immediately hit by a rush of smells and noises that filled her with the thrill of the new and unknown. She blinked at the bright tropical sun and strode forward into the enticing hustle and bustle of Bangkok.
> She didn't really know where her feet were taking her, but she knew that there were a thousand things she wanted to do. Where to begin? The Grand Palace? The market? A stroll along the river? It all had to be done, but the order was open to debate.
> Alice reached in her satchel for her guide book, but she hesitated as her fingers brushed its pages. No, she wasn't going to do this like other people had done it; she was going to do it her way and it'd be all the better for it. Stashing the guide book, she decided that the first adventure would be to follow her eager nose to the market stalls.

a) How is Alice feeling in this extract?

Exited and curious

b) Write out an example from the text that supports your answer.

Smells and noises that filled her with thrill

c) Explain how your example shows how Alice is feeling.

Thrill connotes she is eager to see this new place and is exited by these new smells and noise

d) Now develop your point.

....

....

....

CGP Useless Fact #1872 — a joke can always be made about P.E.E.D. ...

If there's a secret to doing well in English exams, it's probably this: the P.E.E.D. framework is an absolutely brilliant way of writing top-notch answers. It ensures that all of your points are backed up, explained and fully developed. Nifty, eh?

Section One — Exam Basics

Writing Well

Q1 Exam answers should be written in Standard English. For each pair of sentences below, underline the sentence that is written in Standard English.

    a) When all's said and done, the writer in Source A is way more positive about breeding cats.

        Overall, the writer in Source A demonstrates a more positive attitude towards breeding cats.

    b) The writer in Source B doesn't include other people's point of view, so they're very biased.

        The writer in Source B doesn't, like, consider other people's views, so they're really biased.

    c) The writer in Source B tries to get you on side with their own sob story about cat breeding.

        The writer in Source B tries to convince the reader using an anecdote about cat breeding.

Q2 Rewrite each sentence below so that it is in Standard English.

> The metaphor "a furious battleground" suggests that the house is proper chaotic and stuff.

....

....

> When Sam and Nina are talking it tells you how them characters are feeling.

....

....

Q3 Fill in the blanks in the passage below using the explaining words and phrases in the box.

> signifying   furthermore   emphasises   reinforce

> The writer uses short sentences, which increase the pace of the text and build tension. They also help to .... the sense of urgency, and so help the reader to imagine Sadie's panic. .... the setting adds to the suspense. The writer .... the stormy conditions that Sadie is trapped in, ... that she's vulnerable.

Writing Well

Q4   Circle the **four** words and phrases which you could use to link paragraphs in an exam answer.

Another point of view is	Secondly	metaphor	Highlights
Conversely	Safe to say	Don't get me wrong	In addition to this

Q5   Rewrite the following answer. Break it down into **three** paragraphs and add appropriate words or phrases to make the paragraphs link smoothly together.

> The extract from the biography argues that Orson Welles' career was a "magnificent failure". It points to the fact that his greatest achievement, 'Citizen Kane', was made before the age of thirty. The magazine article argues that Orson Welles was a wonderful director and actor throughout his career. It suggests that people like the "myth" of Orson Welles' fall from grace and ignore his later achievements. The third text, the interview with Orson Welles, shows that he himself had conflicting feelings towards his career and achievements. The interviewer describes him as "fiercely proud" of his films, but also "insecure beneath the bravado".

....

....

....

....

....

....

....

....

....

....

....

....

Writing... writing... writing — this writing well has an echo...

Obscure 'well' jokes aside, these pages are full of useful tips for your exam answers. Here's a recap: use Standard English, include a good variety of explaining and linking words or phrases and, whatever you do, don't forget to use paragraphs.

Reading with Insight

Q1   Draw lines to match each passage below with the writer's intended meaning.

a) The sky was a vivacious blue, uninterrupted by cloud
— Claire could imagine exactly how the cool lake
would look beneath it. She crossed another date off
her calendar with a gratifying flick of red marker pen.

**The character is
feeling exhausted.**

b) At last, after an hour spent coaxing the stubborn lever,
Peter's seat reclined. He slowly lowered himself
backwards, finally allowing his drooping eyelids to close.
The sounds of the motorway seemed to instantly lull.

**The character is looking
forward to something.**

c) Suddenly, dishes of every type of cuisine flew in from doors
around the hall, assaulting Tomek's senses and ensnaring
him in a haze of sticky and somewhat nauseating scents.
He reached for his glass of water with a sweaty hand.

**The character is
feeling uncomfortable.**

Q2   Read the following text and then complete the table below.

> The films Alfred Hitchcock made in the 1950s and 1960s contain tantalising
> glimpses of greatness. Iconic images from these films stick in the mind, for example
> Janet Leigh screaming in the shower in 'Psycho'.
>
> However, when looking at Hitchcock's career as a whole, it is his earlier films from
> the 1930s and 1940s which still delight. Early features like 'The 39 Steps' and 'The Lady
> Vanishes' have a wonderful humour and lightness of touch. In contrast, his later films,
> even classics like 'Vertigo' and 'The Birds', are often leaden in their pace and tone.
>
> One reason for the change in quality of Hitchcock's films was the way he gorged
> himself on the worship he received as he got older. Younger film directors like François
> Truffaut revered him. This swelled Hitchcock's already substantial ego, and contributed
> to an increasingly dull, self-conscious style of film.
>
> Pretentious film students might still extoll the virtues of the 'classics', but I'd rather
> watch one of those early, off-the-cuff, Hitchcock masterpieces any day.

Words and phrases which imply the writer dislikes Hitchcock's later films	Words and phrases which imply the writer likes Hitchcock's early films	Words and phrases which imply the writer dislikes Hitchcock as a person
1.	1.	1.
2.	2.	2.

Reading with Insight

Q3   Pick out **one** word or phrase from the text which shows you that the writer wants the restaurant owner to feel apologetic. Then explain why it tells you this.

> I was sorely disappointed last weekend when the standard of food fell well below what I had come to expect from your restaurant. As a loyal and regular customer, I hope you will be forthcoming in providing either reimbursement or a voucher, since I felt cheated in having to pay on this occasion.

Claire wasn't sure what her meal was supposed to be, but she was fairly sure it wasn't the burger she'd ordered.

Example: ....

Explanation: ....

....

....

Q4   Read the following extract:

> Ed shifted his weight from one foot to another and stared through the Saturday crowds, trying to see her among them. She said she'd be here at noon. He checked his phone for the umpteenth time: no messages. He glanced back through the crowds, and of course, there she was, walking right towards him. His stomach churned and he felt his heart beat just a little harder. She caught sight of him, smiled and waved. He couldn't help but grin right back at her. He dug his hand into his pocket and his fingers found the small, velvet box. He was going to do it: he was going to ask her, today at the restaurant. He took a deep breath as she came closer. He didn't want to give himself away.
> "Are you alright?" she asked, having given him a peck on the cheek. "You look a bit peaky."
> "I'm fine," he lied, taking her by the hand. "Happy to see you, of course."

Explain how Ed is feeling in this passage. Give evidence from the text to support your answer.

....

....

....

....

....

I tried to read with insight — I went cross-eyed...

When you read a text, you'll often feel like you just 'know' what the writer's intention is — that's because they've been very clever and made you feel a certain way. The trick is to look more closely at the text to see how they've done that.

Spelling, Punctuation and Grammar

Q1 Put commas and full stops where they're needed into the sentences below.

    a) I jumped out of the taxi narrowly missing a very large puddle by the kerb

    b) Keeley said she wanted a tablet a pair of shoes and some more make-up

    c) As the boat glided past its bright paint glinting in the sun I was able
       to see the captain saluting me his gold braid fluttering in the breeze

Q2 Tick the boxes next to the words that are spelt correctly. Correct the words spelt incorrectly by
putting brackets around each word, crossing it out neatly, and then writing the correction above.

arguement	☐	unnatural	☐	concsious	☐	figarative	☐
neccessarily	☐	disappear	☐	immediately	☐	consience	☐
favorite	☐	embarassed	☐	decieved	☐	occasional	☐

Q3 Copy the sentences below, replacing the full
stops and commas with semicolons, question
marks or exclamation marks where appropriate.

    a) I didn't want to go. The leaden sky threatened rain.

    ....

    ....

As far as time-travel destinations went, the Ice Age had been a poor choice.

    b) Have you ever wondered what it would be like to travel in time. It'd be fantastic.

    ....

    ....

    c) You can come to my party as long as you bring an expensive present, lovingly wrapped,
       stay until the end, which will be 2 am, clear up any spillages, and serve the drinks.

    ....

    ....

    ....

Spelling, Punctuation and Grammar

Q4 Rewrite the sentences below, correcting the grammatical errors in each one.

a) There wasn't no reason to had a fire drill during the exam.

....

b) Hannah should of eaten the sandwich before it's expiry date.

....

Q5 Rewrite the passage below, correcting the **eight** spelling, punctuation and grammar mistakes.

As he stepped out of the exam hall on that tuesday morning, Rashid breathed an enormous sigh of relief. He wouldn't need to do no more practice papers, and his days of revision and stress were finished. He could of shouted with joy. It was over, and hopefuly it had been worth it. He felt the scientific equations evaporates from his mind like morning dew. As Rashid leant gently against the wall to steady himself, he was overcome by the nowledge that his life was now his. He weren't sure exactly what it would bring, but that was part of the excitement

....
....
....
....
....
....
....
....
....
....

I brought a wand to my first spelling lesson — it was all a bit of a let-down...
It was also the day my hopes of becoming a wizard were cruelly dashed... Oh, the harsh lessons of life. Sadly, here's another harsh lesson — poor spelling, punctuation and grammar will cost you marks. Make sure you know your stuff.

Finding Information and Ideas

Q1 Read the text below.

> Dani approached the roller coaster with wide eyes. She had never been a big fan of rides, but her friend Mel had offered to give £20 to charity if Dani agreed to ride the biggest roller coaster in the park — a towering steel beast with four loops and six corkscrew turns. Her stomach churned at the thought.
> "You can do it, Dani," Mel said, squeezing her shoulder. "You might even enjoy it!"

Dani kept insisting she wasn't a big fan, but the rotating blades and constant whirring suggested otherwise.

Tick the **one** statement that is true.

a) Dani's friend Mel loves theme park rides. ☐

b) Dani is nervous about going on the roller coaster. ☐

c) It was Dani's idea to get sponsored to go on the ride. ☐

Q2 Underline the words and phrases which show that the writer has a negative view of the zoo.

> Last weekend we found ourselves with nothing to do on a warm, sunny day, so we decided on a trip to the zoo. The entrance to the zoo was via a rusty iron gate that looked in serious need of repair. We went into the ticket office, only to discover that the floor was filthy; as we looked closer, we realised there was revolting leftover food scattered everywhere. Inside, the animals looked malnourished and miserable in their enclosures, which all seemed dull and empty, with precious little space for them to run around. All in all, a pretty depressing place.

Q3 From lines 3-8 of the text below, write down **three** facts about the garden.

> 1   "If the boiler hadn't broken, we'd have enough money to go to Hawaii by now," said
> 2 Tim glumly, skirting a puddle of mud in order to peg the laundry onto the washing line.
> 3   Alex frowned and sat down heavily on the bench, which took up almost all of the
> 4 space in their tiny back garden.
> 5   "I bet it's sunny there," she said wistfully, pulling her cardigan in closer.
> 6   The wind was whistling a discordant chorus through the gaps in the fence, making
> 7 the damp grass shiver. The gnarled, stunted apple tree in the corner emitted an
> 8 ominously loud groan that made Tim jump.

1) ....

2) ....

3) ....

Finding Information and Ideas

Now you've got the theory sorted, it's time to put it into practice with these exam-style questions.

 Q4 Read the following extract from a novel.

> The doorbell rang. Someone must have answered it, because moments later I heard George's nasal tones in the hallway.
> "So lovely to be here!" he cried, his voice carrying easily across the living room.
> "Did you invite him?" I hissed, staring desperately at Rosa.
> "I could hardly leave him out," she said coolly. "It would have been too obvious."
> He entered the room. His garish purple suit and elaborate hairstyle made him stand out sharply from the other guests. "George, darling," Rosa cooed. "You made it."
> "Rosa!" he said, presenting her with a bottle of cheap-looking wine. "And Freddie," he said to me with a smirk, extending a greasy hand adorned with several gaudy rings. "Good to see you."
> "You too," I said, forcing a smile and letting go of his hand quickly. "Drink?"
> "Oh, go on then," said George, "I'd love a nice whisky, if you have any?"
> "Nothing but the best for you, George," I replied through gritted teeth.

List **four** facts from the text about George.

 Q5 Read the following extract from a review of a holiday park, then tick the **four** statements that are **true**.

> You would need a fortnight to try all the activities at Lowbridge Park. From abseiling to zorbing, the park offers a mind-boggling range of activities. I was only there for a long weekend, so I had to prioritise!
> I began with a pony trek. Although it drizzled the entire morning, it was a great way to explore the woodland. In the afternoon I debated between rock climbing and mountain biking. I settled on the former, primarily to stay out of the rain!
> The next day, the weather was much better, so my choice fell between canoeing and sailing. I settled for a canoe and headed out on the lake, which was simply stunning early in the morning, clear, calm and blue. The good weather lasted into the afternoon, which meant that I was lucky enough to go paragliding. What an exhilarating experience!
> The next morning, I decided to finish my weekend with a spot of archery. Alas, I'm no Robin Hood, but the instructor was patient and funny, and I did improve a little over the course of the morning.

1. The writer went mountain biking. ☐
2. On the second day, the writer got up early. ☐
3. The writer had time to try everything. ☐
4. The writer enjoyed the pony trek. ☐
5. The weather stayed sunny all weekend. ☐
6. You can abseil at Lowbridge Park. ☐
7. The writer liked the archery instructor. ☐
8. The writer went canoeing down a river. ☐

List four reasons why you love studying for GCSE English — umm...

Some questions will simply ask you to find information and ideas in a text. That doesn't sound like too tough a task, but remember that sometimes you'll need to read between the lines a bit — it won't always be dead obvious, I'm afraid.

 ☐   ☐   ☐

Summarising Information and Ideas

Q1 Read the text below.

> "We're going to be late, Samuel," warned Rita, biting her thumbnail nervously.
> "We'll be fine!" insisted Samuel from the depths of his wardrobe. After a moment he emerged, triumphantly holding his favourite leather jacket aloft.
> Rita glared pointedly at her watch, then at Samuel, who grinned.
> "We'll be fine," he repeated, trying on the jacket and admiring his reflection in the full-length mirror.
> "It's bad enough that we have to go at all, and now we're going to show up late too," complained Rita. "This is all your fault. If it were up to me, we'd never have agreed to go. I hated that school."
> "Oh, cheer up, Rita — it's a reunion, not a funeral," said Samuel. "It'll be fun!"

Circle whether each of the following statements refers to Samuel or Rita, then write down a quote on the dotted line to support your choice.

a) The character who is reluctant to go to the reunion. (Samuel / Rita)

....

b) The character who cares most about time management. (Samuel / Rita)

....

c) The more confident character in the extract. (Samuel / Rita)

....

Q2 Summarise the two views given in the text below.

> Human beings have eaten meat for millions of years. Meat eaters argue that we have evolved with the ability to eat and digest meat, proving that it forms a natural part of the human diet. Furthermore, meat contains many vitamins and minerals, particularly iron, that are important for human function.
> However, vegetarians argue that, biologically, we have very little in common with other species of meat-eaters. For example, we lack the ability to kill an animal and take its meat without tools. Additionally, they argue that a high consumption of red meat contributes to a range of health problems in humans, such as cardiovascular disease and some cancers.

Meat Eaters: ....

....

Vegetarians: ....

....

Summarising Information and Ideas

 Q3 Read the following extracts. Source A is a letter written in the 19th century, and Source B is an extract from a diary written in the 20th century.

Source A

Dearest Caroline,

    Lady Jennings and I paid a visit to the slum dwellings today, with a view to helping the children there by investing our funds in a charitable orphanage. I was simply astonished to see the extent of the poverty in which these poor orphans currently live. Of course I had heard that the conditions were unpleasant, but nothing could have prepared me for the destitution I witnessed there. We must do all we can to help these poor, unfortunate souls — it is our duty as their fellow men.

Source B

Dear diary,

    Today I've been helping out at an underfunded local orphanage, which was built for the children who lost their families in the influenza epidemic. It's been really sad to see so many children having to live in such basic conditions, although it's not really that surprising given the state of the area in general.

    They need more support, but even if I had money to give, it shouldn't be my job to help them. Their government should be providing for them better.

Summarise the differences between the writers in Source A and Source B.

 Q4 Read the following extracts. Source A is from a housekeeping magazine written in the 19th century, and Source B is a newspaper article that was written in the 21st century.

Source A

    The secret to a harmonious marriage lies in the willingness of the wife to be amenable to the needs of the husband.

    A good wife will not pester her husband, nor will she bore him with gossip or domestic trivialities. Instead, she will endeavour to be sweet and charming, always fulfilling his needs. If he wishes to complain, she should listen; if he seeks quiet, she should be silent. The home is her sphere, and she should strive to make it a haven for him, in which he need not lift a finger.

Source B

    In the 21st century, a marriage is a partnership of equals. Today, it is common for both members of a couple to work full-time. This means that it is essential for domestic responsibilities to be shared evenly too. Whilst housework was once considered the domain of women, most women today would spurn the idea that they should work full-time and take sole care of a home. Men are just as capable of cleaning and cooking as women, and fortunately many modern husbands have realised this crucial fact.

Summarise the differences between the views given in Source A and Source B.

Summarise the similarities between a raven and a writing desk...

Luckily, you won't be given any Mad Hatter-style riddles in the exam, but comparing texts is an important skill, especially in paper 2. Practice makes perfect — the more you practise identifying differences between texts, the easier it will get.

Audience and Purpose

Q1 For each sentence, circle the word which best describes its intended audience.

a) "Do you yearn for a simpler, more reliable way of managing your finances?"

children / adults

b) "When buying a used car, try to get as much information from the dealer as you can."

experts / novices

When buying a used toilet roll — don't.

Q2 Draw lines to match each text to its main purpose.

a) "Shop around for the best quote — some insurers are much more expensive than others."

To entertain

b) "As the train moved south, first crawling, then increasing to a steady gallop, the scenery gradually changed from the flat and drab to the dramatic and beautiful."

To persuade

c) "Who could disagree with the fact that children should eat healthily?"

To advise

Q3 Find **two** words or phrases that show this text is aimed at a younger audience, and explain how they show this.

Are you looking for a cool summer job?

We've got loads of temporary vacancies with no experience required!

All you need is some free time over the holidays, a positive attitude and plenty of energy. If you've got your own wheels that's even better!

With Spondon Summer Jobs you can:
• gain real-world work experience
• earn a few quid
• make new friends

Whatever you fancy, we can find you a job that suits you down to the ground! Interested? Call Jackie on 0547 262 626 or find us on social media.

Word or phrase: ....

Explanation: ....

....

Word or phrase: ....

Explanation: ....

....

Audience and Purpose

Try these exam-style questions, then use the self-assessment boxes to mark how well you think you did.

 Q4 Read the following extract from a leaflet advertising an aquarium.

> **Come to Oxton Aquarium — you'll have a whale of a time!**
>
> At Oxton Aquarium you can see lots of different sea creatures all in one place. You could be eyed up by an octopus, shaken by a shark or peered at by a pike! They're all here in our very special underwater world — and we're open every day in the school holidays.
>
> Whether you come with your school, your family or your friends, you're bound to have a fantastic time.
>
> "I've had the best day ever. Can we go round again?" — Adam Rodgers, age 9.
>
> Oxton Aquarium is a fun and fishy day out that you'll never forget!

How has the writer adapted their language to engage their audience?

 Q5 Read the following extract from a newspaper opinion piece.

> Is it really that time of year again? The decorations go up and suddenly the nation is whipped up into a frenzy, convinced that the only way to survive the coming holiday is to grab a trolley and raid the supermarket. We stock up as if an apocalypse is coming, buying up vast quantities of everything from over-priced tins of chocolate right down to the last bruised parsnip.
>
> It's time we admitted that the whole process is utterly ridiculous. Don't get me wrong, I love Christmas. I love the decorations, the merriment and, most of all, the abundance of delicious food.
>
> But what simply must end is the bizarre mentality that causes us to frantically race to the shops five minutes before closing time on Christmas Eve. We've all been there, haven't we? Running around like headless chickens, gripped by a sudden and deathly terror that we might not have stockpiled enough after-dinner mints to last the festivities.
>
> Britain, we need to take a stand against festive stress. Christmas is a special time of year; it should be a time to sit back and take a break from the stresses of everyday life. So please, enjoy your holiday — and try to remember that the world won't end should you happen to forget the cranberry sauce.

How does the writer use language to influence their audience?

I took a stand once — I needed something to put my sheet music on...

As it turns out, it's surprisingly difficult to make a living playing the nose flute, but that's beside the point. Audience and purpose are really important in your exam, so use the questions on these pages to really nail your understanding of them.

Informative and Entertaining Texts

Q1   Put an **I** next to the statements that are informative, and an **E** next to the entertaining ones.

  a) "Steven Morrissey was born in Manchester on 22nd May 1959." ☐

  b) "The gig was absolute mayhem. Swathes of bodies ebbed and flowed in a sea
       of delirium — enjoyment and a survival instinct competed for my attention." ☐

  c) "The next event at Spark Bridge village hall is a performance by
       Jim Dodd and the Budgies, at 7.30 pm on December 12th." ☐

Q2   Underline **two** words or phrases in the text below which suggest that its purpose
       is to entertain. Then explain why these examples suggest this on the lines below.

> The woman was incredibly old. Her back was bent permanently by the
> sheer weight of the years she'd lived, and her skin was papery thin, revealing
> a labyrinth of thick blue veins that crisscrossed her trembling hands.
>   She spoke quietly and kindly to the lost child, then, once he had stopped
> crying, gently guided him to sit down on a nearby bench. As they walked,
> the discordant clink and clank of her jewellery sang through the air.

....

....

....

Q3   Read the text below, which is from the travel section of a newspaper.

> Public bathing may not be a familiar experience to a British tourist, but the
> tranquillity of the beautiful Gellért Baths are enough to convert even the most
> apprehensive of travellers. Here, bathers luxuriate across eight thermal pools,
> each of a different temperature. The hottest pool (an immersive 40 degrees)
> soothed my sightseeing-weary muscles as well as any massage I've ever received.

  a) Write down **two** facts about the Gellért Baths that you can learn from this text.

       Fact 1: ....

       Fact 2: ....

  b) Explain how the writer has presented **one** of these facts in an engaging way.

       ....

       ....

Informative and Entertaining Texts

It's time for some more exam-style questions. Remember to use the self-assessment boxes when you're done.

 Q4   Read the following extract from a short story.

> For her thirteenth birthday, Jasmine's parents had bought her a hockey stick. The thought process behind this baffling decision was a total mystery. They should have known better than anyone that she wasn't remotely interested in sport. Wasn't it obvious? She was nearing the point of needing to be surgically removed from her game console, and she had already mastered the art of the forged sick note. Lounging on the sofa was her passion — one to which she dedicated herself with all the staunch tenacity of an Olympic athlete. Going outside with her parents, meanwhile, was more daunting than an icy trek over an arctic precipice. She wasn't at all hopeful for a sudden transformation of her sofa-bound self into a hockey-stick wielding, goal-scoring demon. Those girls terrified her. She was Jasmine the gamer, a silent lone wolf. She was not, nor would she ever be, Jasmine the whooping and cheering team-player.

"The writer is successful in entertaining the reader. She brings the different sides of Jasmine's personality to light."
To what extent do you agree with this statement?

 Q5   Read the following text from a history magazine.

> The Battle of Hastings was fought on October 14th 1066, on a field near Hastings in East Sussex. Led by William the Conqueror, it was the Normans' most important victory over the Anglo-Saxons.
> William's army was a well-trained body of respected fighters. In contrast to Harold's army, which consisted mostly of foot soldiers, William's force had significant numbers of cavalry and archers — the cavalry sat proudly atop horses bred specially for their strength. At the helm of the Norman host stood a man with years of military experience.
> Beginning at around nine o'clock in the morning, the battle was furious and bloody, and vast numbers of soldiers were brutally slain. At one stage, the English, led by King Harold II, were fooled into thinking they had won the battle, so they stormed towards their enemy, only to be mercilessly ambushed and trampled like insects.

© iStockphoto.com/Butsaya

How does the writer use language to both inform and entertain the reader?

Entertaining texts — I thought mobile phones weren't allowed in the exam...
Entertaining and informing are at opposite ends of the spectrum in lots of ways, but they can also be combined. It's really important to keep an eye out for texts with multiple purposes in the exam — they're often the ticket to a good answer.

      Section Two — Reading — Understanding Texts

Texts that Argue, Persuade or Advise

Q1   Draw lines to match each statement below to its purpose.

a) "The barbaric practice of bear-baiting must
be stopped completely and immediately."

To argue

b) "If you want to make a difference, there are
many organisations you can sign up to."

To persuade

c) "By joining our march and signing this petition, you will
be helping to put an end to this disgraceful act of cruelty."

To advise

Q2   Read the following text.

> Flamingos are the most fascinating birds in the world. Their beguiling
> beauty is unrivalled in the animal kingdom. Should such beauty go unsupported?
> I'm starting a vital campaign to sponsor flamingos in zoos. By donating
> just a few pounds, you can help fund the establishment of breeding
> programmes for these most special of birds. The head keeper at my local
> zoo, Jane Sutton, says, "Flamingos really are wonderful animals. A dedicated
> breeding programme would be invaluable to their endurance as a species."

© iStockphoto.com/Anna Omelchenko

The table below shows the techniques used by the writer to persuade the
reader. Fill in the table by picking out examples of each technique.

Technique	Example from text
rhetorical question	
opinion stated as fact	
expert opinion	
direct address to the reader	

Q3   Choose **one** word or phrase from the text below which shows that its purpose
is to advise. Then explain how it helps the writer to achieve this purpose.

> It's easy to get bogged down in all the choices when you're choosing a new mobile
> phone, but don't worry — there are plenty of people out there to help you. You could
> consider going into a phone shop to chat to an expert, or check out a handy online forum.

Example: ....

Explanation: ....

....

Texts that Argue, Persuade or Advise

 Q4 Read the following extract from an advice leaflet about an election.

> ### It's Decision Time — But Who Do I Vote For?
> Unless you've been living under a rock for the past month, you'll probably have noticed that there's an election coming up. Deciding who to vote for can be a daunting task, but it's also an important one. Luckily, there's plenty of help out there.
>
> Firstly, you need to be well-informed on the principles and policies that each party stands for. If you start to feel overwhelmed by all the political lingo in their leaflets, don't panic — have a look online, where there are plenty of websites that break it down for you.
>
> It's also a good idea to look into the candidates in your constituency. They represent you in parliament, so you'll want to vote for someone who has a strong voice, and who will stand up for what your area needs.
>
> It's true — choosing who to vote for isn't easy. However, if you take the time to do a bit of research, you will be able to make the right decision for you.

How does the writer of this text use language to advise the reader?

 Q5 Read the following letter to the editor of the *Daily Muncaster* local newspaper.

> Dear Sir,
>
> I was frankly horrified to read your article about the new soft drink 'Swampy Water' being served in the tuck shop at Muncaster Primary School. This dangerous fad for drinking green, slimy water is clearly idiotic.
>
> Firstly, young children may become confused and think it acceptable to drink real swamp water. I know from my time in the Territorial Army that this would be an ill-advised and perhaps even fatal decision. Secondly, 'Swampy Water' is full of unhealthy sugar and additives — how else would it acquire that lurid green tinge? Finally, the drink is expensive, which means children don't have sufficient funds to purchase the normal, healthy snacks that any sane parent would endorse.
>
> To conclude, it is my firm belief that 'Swampy Water' should be immediately removed from the tuck shop at Muncaster Primary School.
>
> Yours faithfully,
> Gerry Bowness

How does the writer use language to argue that 'Swampy Water' should be banned?

I'm rooting for Teresa Green — her policies woodwork for us all...

Whether it's arguing, persuading or advising, a text's purpose will have a big impact on the way the author writes. To get the most out of your revision, make sure you practise linking a text's purpose to the writer's use of language techniques.

   Section Two — Reading — Understanding Texts

Writer's Viewpoint and Attitude

Q1   Read these play reviews. Write down whether each attitude is **positive**, **negative** or **balanced**.

   a) This playwright's recent offerings on the London stage had established
         high expectations, but his latest "masterpiece" falls far short of that hype.   ....

   b) I have never left a matinee performance and rushed straight
         to the box office to buy a ticket for that evening. Until now.   ....

   c) I can't say I was dazzled, but I certainly wasn't disappointed.
         A pleasant evening, if not one to write home about.   ....

Q2   Draw lines to match the extracts below to the viewpoints they're expressing.

   a) *"I'd be loath to send one of my own
         children to one, but the idea of abolishing
         mixed sex schools entirely is simply absurd."*

   b) *"I've always considered mixed schools to
         be a barrier to educational progress. We
         should all stick with traditional segregation."*

   c) *"Mixed schools are clearly superior,
         but parents should have a choice."*

   d) *"The outdated concept of single-sex
         education has persisted for far too long.
         All education should be gender-blind."*

   i) Prefers mixed schools and thinks
         single-sex schools should be abolished.

   ii) Prefers mixed schools but
         thinks single-sex schools
         should still be an option.

   iii) Dislikes mixed schools but thinks
         they should be offered as an option.

   iv) Dislikes mixed schools and thinks
         all schools should be single-sex.

Q3   Summarise **one** thing that these two writers agree on, and **one** thing that
         they disagree on. Use evidence from the text to support your answer.

Source A Mobile phone disruptions in lessons are a nightmare for any teacher. Surely the best way to prevent this is simply to ban them from school entirely.	**Source B** I'm not about to suggest that students should be permitted to use mobiles during lessons, but I fail to see that any harm can be caused by allowing them during lunchtimes.

The writers agree that ....

....

....

The writers disagree that ....

....

....

Writer's Viewpoint and Attitude

 Q4 Read the following extracts. Source A is from a letter written in the 19th century, and Source B is from a newspaper article written in the 20th century.

Source A
Dear Mr Tinsham,
I read with concern your recent article on the new wave of art reaching British shores. With all due respect, I see it as nothing short of an abomination. It is created with a flagrant disregard for the conventions and traditions of classical art. These 'artists' seem not to have learnt from their predecessors, but instead insist on violating their canvasses with an assault of colour, which to view, in perfect honesty, is simply excruciating.

Source B
The London art scene has rarely been so exciting. We are seeing a real influx of artists who aren't afraid to throw off the iron shackles of 'traditional art' and champion self-expression. They're rule breakers, not intimidated by the giants of the past. They're revolutionaries, constantly looking forward, never back. Only by pushing the boundaries of modern art are we going to see any progression in the medium. When art conforms, it stagnates, and these new experimenters understand that.

Compare how the writers convey their different attitudes towards art.

 Q5 Read the following extracts. Source A is an extract from a diary written in the 19th century, and Source B is from a speech written in the 21st century.

Source A
Dear Diary —
   I've had quite a day today! Daddy and I took a trip to see the new steam train, which was being exhibited in James Square. It was fascinating — a clanking, grinding steel colossus, shiny as a new penny, with a great puff of steam that emerged from its funnel and curled into the summer sky. I've never seen the like — and to think, Daddy says one day they may be able to carry people from one end of the country to the other! I for one cannot wait.

Source B
Residents of Station Crescent! I know that you, like me, are plagued day-in, day-out with the sounds, smells and sights of the railway. Like me, many of you moved here at a time when three or four trains a day passed by, barely disturbing us at all. And like me, you've seen our area systematically invaded by a non-stop army of trains, impacting our quality of life — not to mention the price of our homes. The time has come to take a stand against the relentless growth of the railways.

Compare how the writers convey their different attitudes towards rail transport.

Compare how the students convey their different Attitudes towards exams...

"Student A seems rather miffed that she's stuck indoors revising when she could be outdoors enjoying the sunshine. In contrast, Student B is getting really stuck into his revision material... no, wait, he's just fallen asleep on top of his book."

Literary Fiction and Literary Non-Fiction

Q1 Each of the sentences below use a technique that is common in literary fiction. Label each sentence with the number of the technique used.

    a) The waves whispered to them, the sound of the surf seemed to say, "come in, come in". ....

    b) Somewhere in the house, glass smashed. Cate froze. There were voices downstairs. Strange voices. Someone had broken in. ....

    c) "Didn't you hear?" whispered Farah covertly. "They're going to make you break into the library." ....

1. short sentences for suspense	2. dialogue to move the plot along

3. personification to create atmosphere

Q2 a) Read the literary fiction text below. Underline the words and phrases which suggest the narrator is angry.

> As I stared at the letter, no longer absorbing the words on the page, I realised my hands were starting to shake. How dare they! After all I'd done for that family... their betrayal cut me like a knife. Without even realising it, I'd begun to tear the paper into pieces; ripping, shredding, mutilating the letter until I was left with a pile of limp paper-snowflakes. Then, just for good measure, I aimed a sharp kick at the pile, scattering it across the carpet.

b) Choose one of your answers to **a)** and explain how it shows that the narrator is angry.

....

....

Q3 Use the words in the box to complete the following sentences about literary non-fiction.

purpose   fact   argument   biographies   dialogue   entertain

Literary non-fiction texts are based on .... They include things like travel writing, diary entries and .... Their .... is often to inform the reader or to make an ...., but they also .... They use features such as description and ....

My autobiography is very entertaining, I promise...

Section Two — Reading — Understanding Texts

Literary Fiction and Literary Non-Fiction

After trying these exam-style questions, use the boxes below to tick how well you think you've done.

 Q4 Read the following extract from a novel.

> Annie went from room to room, shaking her head at the disarray. The house looked as if it had been burgled. In the living room, a bookcase had been thrown onto the floor, and paperbacks were scattered chaotically across the carpet. In the kitchen, the floor was a treacherous landscape of smashed crockery and broken glass.
>
> Annie frowned and headed cautiously up the stairs, following the crashing sounds into the master bedroom. Lucas stood with his back to her. His hair was a frantic mess, his movements manic as he pulled every item of clothing out of his wardrobe and launched them behind him. He was muttering frenetically under his breath.
>
> "Lucas," Annie said calmly. He span around, surprised by her presence. His wide eyes were wild, beads of sweat had appeared on his forehead and his cheeks were red.
>
> "I can't find it," he said. "I've looked everywhere. It's lost. They'll kill me."
>
> "Don't be ridiculous. They're not going to kick you out just because you've lost your key to the clubhouse," said Annie, her arms folded.
>
> "What would you know about it, Annie?" said Lucas, his eyes flashing in annoyance. "They're obsessed with not letting any outsiders in. If they find out I've lost it... I'm doomed. Finished. Condemned."

How does the writer bring the characters of Annie and Lucas alive for the reader?

 Q5 Read the following texts about teaching. Source A is from a speech written in the 19th century. Source B is from an autobiography written in the 20th century.

Source A
A schoolmaster must view himself always as a military officer. He must demand respect from his troops, give no ground and yield no position. If he is not thorough, poor discipline and wayward behaviour will surely ensue. When a schoolmaster allows himself to be seen as a friend, all respect is lost. Imparting a meaningful and comprehensive academic education will become impossible. A schoolmaster without control is like a dog without bite.

Source B
As my sepia-toned school-days become steadily more indistinct, the stern face of Mr Wan remains as clear as day. Wan was a firm disciplinarian, and his strict laws meant that I spent much of my adolescent life languishing in detention. But despite the inevitable resentment I felt for him at the time, Mr Wan did give me a lasting education. Not, sadly, in his beloved Chemistry; but certainly in the priceless lesson of human decency. Though my teenage self was unable to see it, Wan listened to me.

Compare how the two writers convey their different attitudes to teaching.

You're writing a book? What a novel idea...

There's a lot to think about when you're reading a literary fiction or non-fiction text — so many literary devices... On the plus side, that gives you loads to write about. Besides, the more you practise identifying this stuff, the less torturous it gets.

19th-Century Texts

Q1 Read the following passage, then answer the questions below.

> Each year, the two families reunite for an agreeable gathering, at which games and cards are played, lively discussions had and much happiness felt by all involved. As the head of the Spears family, Sir Edward frequently begins the proceedings with a short speech, after which his younger brother (whose daughter Catherine, due to her poor health, is often absent from proceedings) proposes a game of cards or croquet to begin the day. The Withers family are historically the victors in games of a physical bent, but owing to an untimely case of influenza on the part of young Albert Withers, the Spears family this year emerged triumphant in all games played.

a) How are Catherine and Sir Edward related?

....

b) Which family won the croquet game this year and why?

....

c) Write down a word or phrase from the text which shows that the families enjoy being together.

....

Q2 Read each of these 19th-century texts, then summarise the writers' viewpoints on the themes below.

> As a gentleman, I find myself honour-bound to bring this matter to your attention. Young ladies of elevated standing, such as Miss Elizabeth, should not be seen walking alone with young men such as Tom Heygate. I think only of her best interests when I warn you of the scandal that could arise from your daughter's association with a mere farmhand.

a) Social class

....

....

> An oppressive silence fills the vast rooms of this house of late: now that my dear Ernest is gone away, they suffer heartily from the absence of his joyful laughter. Regardless, I have done what is necessary, for at school he will learn all that he needs to succeed in life — for that, his foolish mother's heart will learn to endure the ache.

b) Sending children away to boarding school

....

....

19th-Century Texts

Q3 Read the following extract from a letter written in the 19th century.

> Dearest Sophia,
>
>   I hope you know that, as your doting and loving mother, I only ever wish for your good. I do not write to you to chastise, but to beseech you to consider your future. When I heard from your sister that you have been involved in these ghastly 'votes for women' campaigns in London, I came over in a terrible swoon. My darling, a respectable young lady of your age and social standing should not be getting involved in this sort of common and, I daresay, dangerous display. I implore you, for your safety and your reputation, to stay away from these unpleasant protests. If you were, heaven forbid, to be arrested and disgraced, how do you imagine we would ever persuade a young man to marry you? And if you will not consider yourself, at least consider your poor mother. How do you imagine I would survive the shock?
>
>   When I told young Mr Greaves he was deeply concerned, and hoped you would soon be home and away from the perils of the city. He remains, for his part, a very handsome and respectable bachelor. He has recently been promoted at the bank, and I know he would be delighted to receive a note of congratulations from you.

How has the writer used language to try to influence her daughter?

Q4 Read the following extract from a speech written in the 19th century.

> Friends and colleagues, I must first describe my sincerest gratitude for your attendance here today; it is the greatest honour to welcome so many intellectuals into my humble home. Knowing you all to be wise and influential persons, I have asked you here in the hope that we will concur on an issue of great importance.
>
> Gentlemen, you cannot fail to have perceived the overwhelming number of illiterate and uneducated children amongst the poor in our fair city — for when Mother and Father must work in the factories from the break of day until the skies turn dark, who will spare a moment to teach poor Tommy his ABCs? And, lacking this simple knowledge, how can poor Tommy hope to liberate himself from the poverty and crime by which he is surrounded? In ignoring the plight of these small children, we condemn them to a life of hunger and want.
>
> My esteemed friends, the solution to these problems is but a simple one — we must turn our attentions to establishing a unified system of education in this country. I move that we petition our national Parliament to pass a law that will make mandatory a basic education in reading and writing for all young children, be they rich or poor.
>
> This may well be a long fight. Indeed, it may be a difficult fight; but our cause is just and for the greater good of all — and so we must, with all our hearts, persevere.

How has the writer used language to try to persuade the audience?

After a difficult fight with this section, we've persevered to the end...

Yep, you read that right — this page marks the end of Section 2. Don't feel too disappointed though, as there are still four more lovely sections of questions after this one. Up next: a handy dandy section about structure and language.

Tone, Style and Register

Q1 Draw a line to match each sentence to the word that best describes its tone.

a) Forcing captive animals to perform tricks in zoos and circuses is a repulsive and shameful practice that must not be tolerated!

b) Investigators have recently confirmed that DNA found at the scene of the burglary matches that of suspect Fergus Maybach.

c) I had a riot helping out at the birthday party! Who would've guessed that kids were the perfect audience for my magic tricks?

d) As he stared across the bay where they had first met, he remembered vividly the tinkle of her laughter and the floral scent of her hair.

sentimental

detached

angry

upbeat

Q2 For each pair of sentences below, underline the sentence written in a formal register.

a) "Sorry! We don't take credit cards."
"Customers are advised that we do not accept credit cards."

b) "It is essential to ensure you have the correct tools before proceeding."
"Check you've got the proper kit to hand before you go any further."

c) "Rising debts? We've got the info you need to sort your finances out."
"If you have financial complications, contact our trained advisors."

If Gareth knew about one thing, it was style.

Q3 The text below is taken from a travel journal. Write down **three** pieces of evidence from the text that show it has a conversational style.

> At this point I was starting to get a tad — how shall I put it? — cheesed off. It's one thing being patient, accepting the fact that things don't always go to plan and that now and then delays just happen. It's quite another to be told, after paying good money for a ticket to Town A, that for no good reason you're taking a little detour through Village B, River C and Swamp D. I was finding it more and more difficult to follow what I had figured was the local way of dealing with difficulties — smiling and pretending to find the grim industrial scenery interesting. It wasn't.

1) ....

2) ....

3) ....

Tone, Style and Register

Now have a go at these exam-style questions — they will help you to put your knowledge into practice.

 Q4 Read the following extract from a short story.

> Konrad Kaminski whistled as he ambled along the lane, twirling his umbrella acrobatically as he went. Occasionally he played a game with himself, tossing the umbrella lightly in the air and catching it again without breaking his stride.
>
> It had been raining, but now the sun had burst through and was shining triumphantly. The puddles on the road glittered like molten silver, and the grass fields on either side offered up a heady scent of warm, wet earth. Everything radiated spring and promised summer.
>
> It was hard to tell if Konrad Kaminski was absorbing this positivity, or if he too was emitting it. Either way, his pink cheeks and sparkling eyes would have told a passer-by that here was a man for whom anything was possible. And indeed, had this been suggested to him, Konrad Kaminski would have agreed wholeheartedly. For here he was, a reasonably young man in robust health, who had just come into a small fortune, and who had all the necessary intelligence and requisite enthusiasm to make that small fortune into a very large one.

How does the writer use language to create an upbeat tone?

 Q5 Read the following extract from an adventure holiday brochure.

> If you're up to your neck in revision, the promise of a long summer holiday might be the only thing keeping you going. For most students, the dream will be of lazy days spent with mates, maybe playing video games, or getting a bit of a tan down the park. There's nothing wrong with wanting a break. You've earned it. But here at Adventure Action, we can give you the chance to do something unforgettable with your summer.
>
> If you're aged 15 to 18, you could spend four weeks on one of our incredible adventure and conservation programmes at breathtaking locations around the world. You could trek through dense rainforest in Peru, to help build primary schools in isolated villages. You could take a flight over ancient glaciers to volunteer at a remote bear sanctuary in Alaska. Or you could earn a scuba-diving certificate whilst working in a marine biology lab in The Bahamas. Our programmes are tailored to give you a fantastic experience, where you can bag loads of new skills and be a part of something important.
>
> **Adventure beyond the usual this summer. Apply to Adventure Action today.**

How does the writer create a style that appeals to a young audience?

That's the problem with my jokes — they always lower the tone...

When you're reading a text, remember that its tone, style and register have all been carefully chosen by the writer in order to have the maximum impact on the reader. Nothing in a text is random. Unlike platypuses. They're very random.

    Section Three — Reading — Language and Structure

Words and Phrases

Q1   Write the words in the box into the correct columns in the table.

Adjectives	Adverbs
threatening	

~~threatening~~	phenomenal
boastfully	contemptuous
lovely	bitterly
tragically	devotedly

Q2   What does the word 'sneered' suggest in this sentence?

> "Congratulations, Madge," Angus sneered.

....

....

Q3   How does the writer's choice of words create a different impression in each of the sentences below?

> "Just go," she whispered.

> "Just go," she spat.

....

....

....

Q4   How does the author use words and phrases to influence the reader in the sentence below?

> As my dear friend, I am sure you will understand my decision.

....

....

....

....

Words and Phrases

If you're hot on the trail of some exam-style practice, then look no further than the juicy questions below. Afterwards, you can use the boxes at the bottom to say how confident you're feeling with words and phrases.

 Q5   Read the following extract from a short story.

> The wind rose suddenly. It was a bitter wind, a stinging wind, a wind that drowned all thoughts in a roaring cacophony of noise and fury. It was a tempest that barged across the barren, open moorland and threw itself against the stoic stone walls of the cottage. We didn't know when there would be an end to its howling or its persistent, unruly attempts to gain entry into our little home.
>
> We fought back the best we knew how. We had already nailed boards against the window shutters to stop them being wrenched open by the gusts; now we rolled up old rags and laid them against the gaps in the door frames to resist the draughts. Still it savaged us.
>
> "It can't get much worse, can it?" I asked Father, raising my voice above the roar of the enemy outside. His eyebrows drew together sternly.
>
> "We're just going to have to sit it out," he said. "We don't have any alternative."

How does the writer's choice of words and phrases show the effect of the weather?

 Q6   Read the following extract from a piece of fiction.

> She raised an eyebrow at him icily. Her mouth was a stern, straight line. It did not twitch.
>
> "Please," he pleaded, "it was a mistake. It won't happen again."
>
> Her silence was stone cold. He began to wring his hands fretfully. He could feel the sweat prickling like needles on the back of his neck. The seconds crawled by excruciatingly as he waited for her to say something, anything. He briefly considered speaking, but was too fearful of aggravating her further.
>
> "Evidently," she said at last, "you can no longer be trusted." The only emotion in her voice was disdain.
>
> His breath caught painfully in his chest; he knew the worst was coming.
>
> "I have no use for people I cannot trust," she continued. "You are dismissed. Leave now. Resign your post. Never let me see your face again. Understood?"
>
> Trembling, he managed a clumsy nod.
>
> "Good. Now get out."
>
> He turned and, dragging his feet like a condemned man, left the room.

How does the writer use words and phrases to present the characters in this passage?

Words have power — sadly, not the same kind of power as Superman...

The trick here is to get inside the mind of the writer. Writers know what impression they want to create, so they choose their words carefully. If you can work out what effect the writer was aiming for, it's easier to analyse their language.

Metaphors, Similes and Analogy

Q1   Write 'S' next to the similes and 'M' next to the metaphors below.

    a) She was a fraying cable of tension and anger, which could snap at any moment. ....

    b) The glassy eye of the lake watched us in silent judgement. ....

    c) Like a flock of tired ducks, we clustered around our teacher,
        who had brought us snacks to keep us going on the journey. ....

    d) His eyes were hot coals, burning fiercely at the vision he saw before him. ....

Q2   Use the words in the box to complete the following sentence about analogies.

non-fiction	compares	persuade	images

An analogy .... one thing to another. It uses memorable ....

to make something easier to understand. Analogies are often used in ....

texts to try to .... the reader about something.

Q3   Read the texts below. How does the use of an analogy in the second text make it more effective?

A running tap wastes around 6 litres of water for every minute it's left running.	*A running tap wastes the equivalent of seventeen cups of tea for every minute it's left running.*

....

....

Q4   What impression of the sky is the writer trying to create with the metaphors below?

The night sky was a cloth of violet silk scattered with gemstones.

....

....

....

Metaphors, Similes and Analogy

 Q5 Read the following extract from a leaflet about health.

Driving towards a healthier you

If you had a Ferrari, I can only imagine that you would take good care of it. You might only fill its tank with premium fuel. You might have it regularly serviced. You would take pride in it, polish it at the weekends and keep the upholstery clean.

If you would take this much care of a Ferrari, surely you should take this much care of your body? After all, it's the only one you're ever going to have — you can't just trade this engine in if it breaks down. This means you should fuel yourself properly, eating regular meals that are full of the vitamins and minerals needed for optimum human performance. Keep your body's systems working effectively by exercising regularly and getting plenty of fresh air. And finally, take pride in your body: if you're striving to be happy and healthy, that is something to celebrate.

Regardless of shape or size, your body is priceless — and that's more than you can say for a luxury sports car, isn't it?

How does the writer use an analogy to try to influence the reader?

 Q6 Read the following extract from a piece of fiction.

The landscape was dull steel. The sea was grey, the sky was grey and the mountains in the distance were grey. And we were grey too. Our meagre rations of bread and nameless slop had left us sallow-faced, with dark rings under our eyes. We huddled together nervously, like mice in a cage. A thin layer of snow carpeted the tundra already. It was only September; there would be plenty more snow to come. The wind whipped at our cheeks and we shivered.

The soldiers were smoking by the hut, casting sideways glances at us once in a while, to make sure that we weren't doing anything foolish, like trying to escape. Eventually they trampled on their cigarettes and marched over to us — wolves in military uniform, coming to snarl at lambs.

"There's work to do!" the officer in charge barked, clapping his gloved hands and then gesturing to the crates we'd unloaded. "Come on! Get a move on!" He fired his orders like cannon balls, and we dispersed frantically to do as he said. "If they're not all unpacked by nightfall, no one eats."

How does the writer use metaphors and similes to bring this scene to life for the reader?

Sometimes, revising is like banging your head against a brick wall...

Get the differences between similes, metaphors and analogies clear in your mind. Once you know what you're looking for, it becomes much easier to spot them in texts — but always remember to comment on how they affect the reader.

    Section Three — Reading — Language and Structure

Personification, Alliteration and Onomatopoeia

Q1   For each extract, circle the technique being used.
Then explain **one** effect that the technique creates.

"Eat me... Eat me!"

© iStockphoto.com/unalozmen

a)   "The computer grumbled into life, before smugly informing
me that it was starting on six hours of updates."

Personification / alliteration / onomatopoeia

....

....

....

b)   "The buzz and chatter of the students ruined the tranquillity of the scene."

Personification / alliteration / onomatopoeia

....

....

c)   "Bag a Bargain at Brigson's — Portsmouth's Premier Pig Farm!"

Personification / alliteration / onomatopoeia

....

....

Q2   Underline **one** example of personification and **one** example of alliteration
in this advert, then explain their effect on the reader on the lines below.

A Call for Heroic Hikers!

Are you a fearsome fell-runner? Or maybe you just enjoy long strolls
through the hills? Whatever your ability, we want you to sign up for our
40-mile Wilderness Walk, taking place in the mountainous forest above
Tennerton. If you train hard, you'll not only get fit, but triumph over a
challenging foe and raise lots of money for charities in the local area.
To answer the cry of the hills and get involved, visit the council's website.

© iStockphoto.com/peangdao

Effect of personification: ....

....

Effect of alliteration: ....

....

Personification, Alliteration and Onomatopoeia

And now, here's some handy exam-style practice for writing about these three language techniques.

 Q3 Read the following extract from a short story.

> It was dark in the forest, and eerily close. Even small sounds were amplified into threatening noises. They heard the sinister creaking of the branches; the furtive rustle of leaves; the cracking of a twig that set their hearts racing. And every time they looked behind them, they were sure the scene had changed. Had that fallen log been there before? Had they really not seen that stream? It was as if the forest was playing tricks on them — purposefully trying to deceive and confuse them. Shadows seemed to shift, skipping about the forest floor, delighted at the predicament of the lost wanderers.
>
> Suddenly they heard a shrill screech. It pierced their ears and stopped them dead. The noise rang out again and they squinted upwards to see a large but haggard owl perching on a branch, staring down threateningly. It was guarding the path ahead.

How does the writer use onomatopoeia and personification to describe this scene?

 Q4 Read the following extract from a piece of travel writing.

> The streets of Kuala Lumpur are a labyrinth of lost lanes, back-streets, dead-ends and alleys, which twist and turn and double back on themselves, constantly trying to bewilder the unaccustomed traveller. An apparently infinite series of haphazard side streets break out from the main street of the Chinatown area, like snakes winding across the desert. On every corner hang the pungent but irresistible smells of food stalls offering a cornucopia of exotic cuisines. Heavy trucks rumble past impatiently, whilst thousands of scooters whine and buzz like a swarm of bees, honking horns and hurling out exhaust fumes that stubbornly stagnate in the desperately hot air. The heat is relentless. Even standing still in the shade I can feel the sweat gathering on my forehead.
>
> In search of a bit of peace from the incessant heat and choking fumes, I make my way to the city centre park. Here, neat pathways wind their way leisurely through immaculate green lawns. On every side of the park, glimmering steel skyscrapers tower into the sky, peering down at the people walking below. It's like being surrounded by a giant metal rainforest, thronging with life.

How does the writer use alliteration, onomatopoeia and personification to convey their attitude to Kuala Lumpur?

The workbook eyed me scoldingly, nagging me to get on with revision...

Whenever you're looking at a piece of descriptive writing, whether it's from a work of fiction or non-fiction, you're bound to find a few examples of these literary devices. Some, like onomatopoeia, you probably use yourself without even noticing.

      Section Three — Reading — Language and Structure

Irony and Sarcasm

Q1 Use the words in the box to complete the following passage about irony and sarcasm.

offence	intended	humour	opposite	cruel	context

Irony is when a piece of writing says the .... of its .... meaning.

The reader can tell that the writer is being ironic because of the .... Irony is

often used to add .... to a text. Sarcasm, on the other hand, is intended to cause

.... It uses irony with a .... tone to make fun of someone or something.

Q2 Tick which of the extracts below is sarcastic, then give an example and explanation to support your answer underneath.

> Ivan is a responsible lad with a keen sense of innovation. He's not afraid to embrace change, and he takes action where necessary without needing constant support. He can be forgetful at times, but overall he looks to be a worthy addition to the company. ☐

> Oh yeah, Ivan is a brilliant secretary — I especially appreciate the way he keeps forgetting to bring a pen and steals mine instead. And he's reorganised our files into a brand new system, which only he can understand — that's really made our lives easier. ☐

....

....

....

Q3 How does the writer use irony to show the characters' attitudes in the extract below?

> "You're so lucky to have made it as an actor," Gemma sighed.
> "You're well-paid, you travel the world, you meet all the celebrities..."
> Maya smiled. "It's a trial, that's for sure."
> "Oh yes, you clearly suffer for your art!" Gemma laughed.

....

....

....

....

Irony and Sarcasm

 Q4 Read the following extract from an opinion column in a newspaper.

> ## SATISFACTION GUARANTEED!
>
> The other day I had to phone up my insurance company with the horrendously complicated problem of changing my address. After spending twenty thrilling minutes on hold, listening to a variety of boy bands performing their classic hits, I finally got through to the man on whom my lofty ambition rested — Brendan.
>
> However, there was a slight hitch. It seems that, for such a highly skilled telephone operative as young Brendan, a task which may appear simple to us mere mortals must in fact be performed with studious precision. Fortunately, his professionalism shone through as he kept me informed that some "technical stuff had gone weird". This was obviously of great comfort to me, as I watched night-time slowly approach and began to revise my plans for what was left of the week.

How does the writer use irony and sarcasm to convey their attitudes to their insurance company?

 Q5 Read the following extract from a piece of fiction.

> "Have a good time at Kirsty's!" Hafsa's father called from the car, as he dropped her off at my house.
>
> "Oh, we'll have a great time," she said, but rolled her eyes at me as soon as her dad pulled away. It really was going to be a fun-filled night; we had maths homework, physics homework and French homework to do for the next day. Coming up to exams, it seemed like the fun never stopped.
>
> We settled down on my bedroom floor with a bowl of popcorn for sustenance. Hafsa opened up the maths textbook and read aloud.
>
> "Find the coordinates of the minimum point of the graphs of each of the following equations."
>
> I groaned.
>
> "Fantastic," Hafsa said, "a nice easy one to start one with. Thanks Miss Hayward, you're a real friend to students."
>
> "Compassionate and fashionable," I said with a smirk. "Did you see what she was wearing today?"
>
> "What, that medieval blouse thing? Very on trend." We both laughed.

How does the writer use irony and sarcasm to present Hafsa and Kirsty?

Sarcasm — some say it's the lowest form of wit...

Remember that irony is less condescending than sarcasm. Because sarcasm tends to be nasty, it says as much about the person using it as the person or thing it's directed towards — something to bear in mind when you're analysing texts.

     Section Three — Reading — Language and Structure

Rhetoric and Bias

Q1 Draw lines to match each sentence to its technique.

a) Nothing is more disgusting than a mouldy sandwich.   **antithesis**

b) The sandwich, which had been in the fridge for
at least a fortnight, was disgustingly mouldy.   **parenthesis**

c) Far from the sandwich heaven I'd been hoping
for, I found myself in sandwich hell.   **hyperbole**

Q2 Underline **one** rhetorical technique in this passage. Then, on the lines
below, name the technique and explain the effect on the reader.

> *Who has not felt outraged at the injustice of the world when viewing images of
> child poverty? We live in a world where millions of children must battle with
> hunger, thirst and poor sanitation every day. Your donation, if you can find it in
> your heart to give one, will truly change these children's lives for the better.*

Technique: ....

Effect: ....

....

....

Q3 Explain why the following text is biased. Use
evidence from the text to support your answer.

> By far the best hobby for young people is the card game "cribbage". All
> young people from the ages of eight to eighteen adore playing cribbage.
> It's easy to learn, doesn't need much equipment and provides hours of fun.

....

....

....

....

Rhetoric and Bias

If you need to write about rhetoric or bias in your exam, these exam-style questions will help you prepare.

 Q4   Read the following extract from a travel brochure.

> Everyone daydreams. When you're stuck in the office — dealing with tricky customers, struggling with spreadsheets, drinking tepid tea — have you ever dreamt of turning your back on the daily drudge and escaping on a luxury break? Well, look no further than Malliwest Holidays — offering the best range of exclusive package holidays for the discerning traveller.
>
> Perhaps your perfect escape features breathtaking Arctic scenery? If so, let us take you on an adventure to Iceland. Here you can be astounded by the otherworldly Northern Lights; you can luxuriate in the world-famous volcanic hot springs; and you can embark on one of our expertly guided whale watching tours.
>
> Or perhaps your idea of adventure is a five-star African safari? Malliwest's safari camps in Kenya offer accommodation in lavish tent complexes, with stunning views over the national park and the services of expert wildlife rangers, who will bring you face to face with animals such as lions, zebra and gazelle.
>
> And if relaxation is what you need, then rest assured that our top-end, all-inclusive beach resorts will satisfy your every desire. From private, white, sandy beaches to stunning infinity pools; from complimentary cocktails to Michelin-starred dining facilities; from award-winning spas to no-expenses-spared suites; your every wish will be catered for by our dedicated, professional staff.
>
> We can't wait to welcome you on your well-deserved break.

How does the writer use rhetorical devices to try to persuade the reader?

 Q5   Read the following extracts. Source A is from a letter written in the 19th century, and Source B is from a review posted on a travel website in the 21st century.

Source A	Source B
Dear Jane, I have arrived at my lodgings in Ware. They are satisfactory, if not impressive — the room must once have been decorated in good taste, but alas, it is the good taste of a bygone age. Nevertheless, the room is clean, tidy and of a good size. As I had expected, the mattress was not of the standard I am accustomed to (nor, for that matter, was the limited refreshment offered by the kitchens), but for a short stay, it will suffice.	The room smelt like its window hadn't been opened for about a century. The wallpaper was peeling. The carpet was a battlefield between all sorts of suspicious stains. Given the state of the rest of the room, I doubted that the 'fresh' bedding was clean, but it was the mattress that really drew my attention — it was like something from a Victorian prison cell, barely a few inches thick.

Compare how the two writers have conveyed their attitudes to their rooms.

Homework is the worst thing ever — students swear that's not hyperbole...

When I tell you that learning this stuff is really important, I'm not exaggerating. Understanding bias and the rhetorical devices on these pages will really help you to write specific (and impressive) analysis about texts. Sounds good to me.

Descriptive Language

Q1   Use the words in the box to complete the following sentences about descriptive writing.

> agree   engaging   build   contrasting

Descriptive writing makes a text .... for the reader.

A writer can .... an overall description throughout

a text, by using sentences with .... descriptions or

descriptions that .... with each other.

There was sand. And more sand. That's all I've got.

Q2   Find an example in the extract below of each of the following descriptive techniques.

> The air smelt of scorched grass. I could feel the blistering sun burning into my skin as I trudged slowly through the prickly, dry vegetation, my heavy load cutting cruel lines into my drooping shoulders. In the distance, the air shimmered in waves with the heat. I felt as if I were underwater, constantly being pulled back by the tidal drag of the temperature, every step an effort, every breath a trial.

Descriptive adjectives: ....

Describing different senses: ....

Descriptive verbs: ....

Imagery: ....

Q3   Circle which extract is the better example of descriptive writing and explain your answer using examples from the text.

i)
> *My first football match was great. The sights and sounds were amazing.*

ii)
> *I remember my first football match so clearly: the sound of the fans as loud as ten jet engines; the emerald green pitch; and the buzzing, electric atmosphere. I'll never forget it.*

I think extract **i) / ii)** is the most descriptive because ....

....

....

....

Section Three — Reading — Language and Structure

Descriptive Language

 Q4 Read the following extract from a novel.

> He decided to visit the old railway station down the road from where he grew up. It was abandoned now, but the smell of diesel still clung to the walls. It was eerily quiet. The only sounds were the ghostly creaking of the rusted platform signs, and the rustle of litter as the wind blew it across the warped tracks. He wandered down a desolate platform towards the old footbridge. The grey, rusty girders seemed to sag under the weight of memories.
>
> Once, this station had been a bustling interchange; commuters in smart suits had skipped on and off trains, newspapers nestled smartly under their arms, sleek briefcases clutched in their hands. Conductors in their pressed uniforms, with shining brass buttons and gleaming silver whistles, had seen each train off on its journey with a congratulatory wave. He remembered the thundering noise of an approaching train echoing down the track like the roar of some terrific beast; the clatter of footfalls on the steel steps as people hurried to make their connections.
>
> Now there was no one — just him, paying his respects like a visitor to a grave.

How does the writer use descriptive language to show contrasts in this extract?

 Q5 Read the following extract from a short story.

> "Howard, you made it!" Percy beamed, ushering me through the doors of his mansion. "Come in, come in — you don't want to miss a minute of this party; I promise you, it's my best yet!"
>
> He hastened me through the marble hallway towards the ballroom. I could already hear the thumping of music and the hum of voices. As the golden doors were opened, the noise hit me like a wave. The room was thronged with hundreds of guests, and they were all joking, laughing, making introductions. Their voices wove together into a single, undulating buzz of talk. Beyond their voices was the exuberant playing of the live band; drums and saxophones adding bass and melody to the already throbbing noise. There were other sounds too — the clinking of glasses, the occasional popping of champagne corks followed by cheers.
>
> And the colours! The men were all in tuxedos, cutting sharp lines of white and black, while the women were shimmering in silks of every colour — emerald and scarlet, gold and violet, cobalt and cerise. Lights glittered from the chandeliers, sparkling on the women's jewellery and the martini glasses and the silverware. The ballroom had become a never-ending kaleidoscope of wealth.

"The writer of this extract uses descriptive language very successfully. The reader really feels like they're at the party with Howard."
To what extent do you agree with this statement?

I'll describe myself — good looking, smells of roses, voice like an angel...

A great description really makes a piece of writing. In your exam, try to comment on the effect of specific techniques — like similes, metaphors and descriptive words and phrases — as well as the overall impression that the description creates.

Narrative Viewpoint

Q1 Use the words in the box to complete the following sentences about narrative viewpoint.

| first-person | detached | perspective | third-person | personal |

The narrative viewpoint is the narrator's .... on the text. A

.... narrator is not one of the characters, so they describe the characters

using words like 'he' and 'she'. This type of narration is more ...., as it

is separate from the characters.

A .... narrator will tell the story using words such as 'I' and 'me'.

This creates a very .... link between the reader and the narrator.

Q2 For each extract below, write whether it uses a first-, second- or third-person narrator.

a) The detective couldn't help but admire the thieves' handiwork. ....

b) We crouched behind the sofa, trembling with fear. ....

c) "I don't remember," she said, but a memory was stirring in her mind. ....

d) You hurry down the dark street, heart thudding, head spinning. ....

e) "You have to run," I whispered urgently, "they'll be here soon." ....

Q3 Explain why using a first-person narrator is effective in the extract below. Use evidence from the text to back up your answer.

> They told me I was in safe hands. They told me I wouldn't feel a thing. And I knew I should believe them. But lying there on the operating table, with the nurses and doctors swarming around my head in their clinical white uniforms, like scientists around a lab rat, all I could feel was terror. One of them grinned at me reassuringly, and I pasted a smile on my face in return, but inside I felt as if someone had filled my gut with ice, and I could feel a cold sweat breaking out on my palms.

....

....

....

....

Narrative Viewpoint

Q4 Read the following extract from a piece of fiction.

> It is very late and the train is quiet. There are only four passengers in the carriage. The first is a young man in a smart but cheaply-made suit. He has just been to his first job interview and is nervously and repeatedly checking his mobile phone.
>
> The second passenger is a middle-aged woman with greying hair. She is propped up against a window, fast asleep. She has three jobs at the moment, and together they just about pay the bills, but she spends her life in a constant state of exhaustion.
>
> The final two passengers are a retired couple, who have just been to visit their young grandchildren. The woman is feeling glad that she and her husband live over an hour away, and aren't asked to babysit more often. She had forgotten how exhausting babies were. Her husband had been thinking something similar, but is now wondering if the weather will be good enough for a round of golf tomorrow.
>
> None of the passengers in the carriage take much notice of one another. None of the passengers in the carriage are aware that a murder has been committed on their train, and that by the time they pull in at their destination, they will all be suspects.

How does the writer use narrative viewpoint to bring all four characters to life?

Q5 Read the following extract from a short story.

> I'm not a hero. I just did what I had been trained to do. Any other air-raid warden would have done exactly the same. And besides, I was heading over to Mrs White's house anyway. The air-raid sirens had already sounded, and most people were already tucked away in shelters. But my wife was good pals with Mrs White, so I knew she was in bed with a chest infection, and had planned to stay there if the sirens sounded. We'd had countless air-raid warnings, and very few bombs, so you can understand why a poorly woman with three kiddies might decide to chance it in her own home for a night, can't you?
>
> Then I heard them. Bombs dropping. They were ground-shaking booms, distant at first, but then closer. My heart was in my throat, I can tell you. There was a haze of orange firelight in the sky. I stood in a doorway, not knowing where the next one would hit. It came down right ahead of me. The explosion threw me back against the door, and my ears started ringing as glass from blown-out windows rained down into the street. I could see the flames, and I knew that they were coming from near Mrs White's house. I ran there as best I could, though I was still pretty shaky. When I got there, I saw that her neighbour's house had been completely destroyed by the bomb. Gone, just like that. Hers was still standing, but in a real bad way. I could see it was filling up with smoke. But I knew there were kids in there, so I didn't think twice. "Buck up, Harry," I thought, and I ran in to see if I could help them.

How does the writer use narrative viewpoint to describe Harry?

I know why they call it the first person — because I'm number one...

Alas, identifying if a text uses the first, second or third person is usually the easy part of the exam. The harder part is trying to understand *why* the author has chosen a particular viewpoint — you'll need to write about the effect that it has.

Section Three — Reading — Language and Structure

Structure — Whole Texts

Q1 Draw lines to match each structural technique with its definition.

a) **Cinematic writing**

b) **Non-linear writing**

c) **Perspective shifts**

d) **Linear writing**

i) When the point of view of a text moves between different characters and/or locations.

ii) Writing where the text is written as if the reader is watching a film.

iii) Writing that tells the events of a story in chronological order.

iv) Writing that tells the events of a story in a non-chronological order.

Proof that structure is important.

Q2 Read the extract below.

> It was one of those frosty winter mornings. The sky was a clear forget-me-not blue, and the grass stood rigid and silver with frost. Robins chirped proudly as they flittered in and out of the glittering bramble bushes. The kitchen sang with the smell of hot, buttered toast and fried bacon. A large, red pot of tea sat on the kitchen table, steam curling from its spout.

Cross out the incorrect word from each pair of bold words.

a) This extract opens with **description / dialogue**.

b) This means that the reader's focus is initially on the **setting / characters**.

c) It moves the reader's attention from **outside / inside** to **outside / inside**.

Q3 Read the extract below and then complete the sentence using words from the box.

> I put the hot chocolate in front of Alice, and waited for her to finish crying. She wiped her eyes with a tissue and looked up at me blearily.
> "I'll tell you what happened," she said, and took a breath. "It all started last week, when Robyn and I came out of the cinema. We bumped into Hayley and Dan, and we all decided to go for lunch together, to that new burrito bar that's opened in town..."

characters	move	frame	story	multiple

This is an example of a .... narrative — there is a ....

within a story. This type of narrative allows writers to .... the

readers' focus between .... settings and ....

Structure — Whole Texts

Q4 This is the ending to a short story. Joan is eighty-six years old, and one of the nurses from her care home has volunteered to take her to the beach.

> They arrived shortly before lunchtime. The seagulls squawked noisily overhead, swooping and circling, bright as doves against the blue sky. The nurse pushed the wheelchair down the boardwalk. Looking out over the sand and the grey-green sea, Joan was transfixed.
>
> The first time she had been to the beach was as a little girl, shortly before the war broke out. It had been a hot day. The beach was full of people sprawled on multicoloured deck chairs and picnic blankets, lending the scene a carnival feel. She remembered the smell of the water as she raced into the sea for the first time. She remembered the feeling of damp sand between her fingers and toes, and how the sea salt had dried into tiny crystals on her skin. Her mother had packed a picnic of hard-boiled eggs and potato salad. It had been the best day of her life so far, and as her father had bundled her into a towel, tired and sun-soaked, ready to go home, she had already been looking forward to the next visit.
>
> Now Joan watched the children race delightedly across the sand like she had done. Her nurse bought her fish and chips for lunch. Joan bought sticks of rock for her great-grandchildren. As the sun was going down, and they headed back to the car, Joan looked back over her shoulder. She knew there wouldn't be a next visit — but she didn't mind. She had seen the sea again.

How has the writer structured the text to interest you as a reader?

Q5 Read the following extract from the opening of a short story.

> The noise was deafening. In the village hall, a children's party was in full swing. Pop music blared through the speakers. There was screeching and laughing and the mad rush of running footsteps rocketing from one side of the room to the other as games were played. Rainbow-coloured balloons and shimmering banners hung from the ceiling. A generous pile of presents in bright wrapping paper stood in one corner. The remnants of a buffet lurked in another — half-eaten sausage rolls and sweet wrappers mingled among dirty paper plates. And there, sitting cross-legged underneath the buffet table, was a little boy with enormous, mournful brown eyes.
>
> Like the other kids at the party, the boy was dressed in his best clothes: shiny white trainers, and jeans without holes in the knees. He was chewing his bottom lip, his hands folded neatly in his lap, watching the other children play. It wasn't that the boy didn't want to join in — he did, more than anything else. But the other kids called him names, and ran away from him. The boy knew why they avoided him. The problem was that he simply wasn't like the other kids. He wasn't like the other kids at all.

How has the writer structured the text to interest you as a reader?

This workbook is structured so that you ace your exams...

Both fiction and non-fiction texts are structured for maximum effect. Non-fiction is often structured to make its content clear, or to have a persuasive effect. Fiction can be structured to engage the reader in its events, settings or characters.

Sentence Forms

Q1 Label each sentence below as either simple, compound or complex.

a) Gazing longingly out to sea, the sailor dreamed of adventure. ....

b) I waited for an hour, but he never arrived. ....

c) She listened in shock to the news on the radio. ....

d) He never imagined that people could live in such poverty. ....

e) The sun rose reluctantly, casting sombre shadows across the fields. ....

f) Night was closing in fast, so we needed to find the path soon. ....

Q2 The four sentences below say a similar thing in different ways.

a) | *Bullying in schools is a serious problem.*

c) | *Haven't you had enough of bullying?*

b) | *Stop bullying today.*

d) | *We must stop bullying!*

For each sentence, identify the type of sentence using the options in the box, then explain why a writer might have chosen each one. The first answer has been done for you.

| ~~statement~~ | exclamation |
| question | command |

a) Sentence type: ...*statement*...

Using a clear statement makes the writer sound serious and objective. The writer might have chosen to use a statement to emphasise that bullying is a serious topic.

b) Sentence type: ....

....

....

c) Sentence type: ....

....

....

d) Sentence type: ....

....

....

Sentence Forms

Now you've covered different sentence forms, have a go at these longer questions to put your knowledge to good use. Then tick a box at the bottom of the page to show how you did.

 Q3 Read the following extract from a piece of fiction.

> The theatre hummed with expectant conversation as the spectators began to fill the stalls. The red velvet seats and gentle golden lighting gave the impression of being caught in the centre of a giant ruby. There was a magical feeling, as if everyone knew they were going to witness something spectacular that night, and eyes kept flickering over to the theatre drapes, wondering when the show would begin.
>
> Backstage, biting his fingernails down to the nail-bed, was the one they were all waiting for. Mikhail had been told by everyone he met that he was the greatest tenor of all time. Conductors had shed a tear when he sang, audiences had wept openly. But that never stopped him from feeling sick with nerves before a performance. What if his voice faltered? What if he forgot the words? What if he disappointed them all?
>
> "Sixty seconds to curtain," the stage manager called to him. Mikhail took a deep breath. His palms were damp with sweat. His legs felt like jelly. He didn't know if he was ready for this.

How has the writer used different sentence forms to create tension?

 Q4 Read the following extract from a piece of fiction.

> The shot rang out. Jane powered off the blocks. The sound of the stadium had faded now, and only one thing mattered: putting one foot in front of the other, faster than she had ever done before. This was her race. She was born for this! Her blood pounded in her ears as she sprinted round the track.
>
> In the distance, the finish line was approaching. There were still two runners ahead of her. Faster! Jane urged herself on. Her legs burned. Her lungs screamed. But she was gaining on them. She overtook one. Still faster! At the last second, she overtook the final competitor and her foot came down first, landing triumphantly over the white line.
>
> Jane slowed to a halt, and doubled over with her hands on her knees as she gasped for breath. Wiping the sweat from her eyes, she looked up again at the stadium, and nearly cried with joy. Thousands and thousands of people were on their feet, cheering; they were waving flags and calling her name, smiles reaching from ear to ear. She could hardly believe it. All the months of hard training had paid off and she had achieved her lifelong dream: she had won a gold medal at the Olympics.

How has the writer used different sentence forms to engage the reader?

"And your sentence shall be — two hours of revision! Mwah ha ha..."

Sentences might seem easy enough, but they're fundamental to a piece of writing. It's worth taking the time to perfect your skills at analysing them closely. Ask yourself *why* the sentence has been written like it has, and think about its effects.

Writing with Purpose

Q1 Put each of the following writing techniques into the appropriate column of the table, depending on whether they're more common in informative or persuasive writing.

an impersonal tone	rhetorical questions	technical terms	emotive language

Informative writing	Persuasive writing

The leader of the 'no to school uniforms' campaign was a formidable opponent.

Q2 Complete this brief plan to show how you would structure a speech arguing in favour of school uniforms.

Introduction: *Clearly outline the main points of the argument.* ....

1) ....

2) ....

3) ....

Conclusion: ....

Q3 Rewrite the informative text below so that it persuades the reader to visit the church.

Lyttlewich Church

Situated in the rural village of Lyttlewich, Howtonshire, Lyttlewich Church is one of the oldest churches in the country: some parts of the church were built in 984 AD. The church receives thousands of visitors a year, and is particularly renowned for its artwork, which has recently been restored.

....

....

....

....

....

Writing with Purpose

If you've mastered those short questions, here are some exam-style questions to have a crack at.
When you're done, tick a box at the bottom of the page to show how you got on with the whole lot.

 Q4 Answer the exam-style question below.

> One of your classmates has said: "I think going to bed early is a waste
> of time. All the good television programmes are on late at night."
>
> Write a speech in which you try to persuade your class
> that it's important to get a full night's sleep.

 Q5 Answer the exam-style question below.

> "Young people need to learn how to express themselves. Creative subjects
> such as Art and Drama should be compulsory for all students aged 5-16."
>
> Write a speech to be given to your school governors in
> which you argue your point of view on this statement.

 Q6 Answer the exam-style question below.

> You are going to enter a creative writing competition. Your entry will be
> judged by a panel of professional authors, who will be judging you based
> on how entertaining your writing is.
>
> Write the beginning of a story suggested by this picture:
>
>

Purr, puss... there's a joke in there somewhere...

It's really important to keep your purpose in mind when you're answering question 5 in each paper. As part of your exam
preparation, make sure you practise spotting the purpose in this type of question, then adapting your writing to match it.

Writing for an Audience

Q1 Rewrite each sentence below so that it's appropriate
for an audience who have no expertise on the subject.

a) "Fertilisers provide phosphorus and potassium, which are essential for plant growth."

Fertilisers provide things that plants need to grow.

b) "The ossicle bones in the ear (the malleus, incus and stapes)
are some of the smallest in the human skeleton."

....

c) "Roman legionaries used javelins and throwing-darts to defeat their enemies."

....

Q2 Write down a good opening sentence for each of the texts below.
Make sure it's suitable for the audience given in the question.

a) An article for a teenage magazine, in which you say that schools should
spend more time teaching students how to manage their money.

....

....

b) Instructions for a primary school student to teach them how to bake a cake.

....

....

Q3 The extract below is from a letter written to a familiar audience.
Rewrite it on the lines below as if you were writing to a local newspaper.

> The quality of the fresh fruit in the shops around here is
> ridiculous — I couldn't find a decent apple anywhere!

....

....

....

Writing for an Audience

Q4 Answer the exam-style question below.

> You want to write a story to give to one of your friends for their birthday. Your friend is the same age as you.
>
> Write a short story suggested by this picture:
>
>

Q5 Answer the exam-style question below.

> "Young people are often unaware of the dangers they face when crossing roads. It is absolutely crucial that we teach young people to be aware of this danger."
>
> Write a speech for an audience of students in your year group, in which you argue your opinion on this statement.

Q6 Answer the exam-style question below.

> You have been asked to write a piece for a storytelling event at your local library. Your writing will be read aloud to an audience of adult library users.
>
> Write the beginning of a story about somebody who goes camping.

I hypnotise my audience to keep their attention...

You are feeling sleepy... very sleepy... and on the count of three, you'll be able to answer every question in this book with great ease... Ah, if only it were that simple. Sadly, the only way to get the hang of writing questions is to practise. Lots.

    Section Four — Writing — Creative and Non-Fiction

Writing Stories

Q1 Use the words in the box to complete the following sentences about how to begin a story.

> attention   middle   clichés   character   engage   direct

Stories need to immediately .... the reader. This is

often achieved by starting a story in the .... of the

action or by introducing an unusual .... Stories

can also use .... address to grab the reader's

.... — but they need to avoid ....

By the sixteenth read-through, Clara's favourite story was starting to grate on Ron.

Q2 Imagine you are going to write a short story about somebody who's lost in a forest.

a) What narrative viewpoint would you use? Give a reason for your answer.

....

....

b) Write down two descriptive adjectives you could use, and explain their effect.

....

....

c) Write down a simile you could use.

....

Q3 Write the closing sentences for each of the stories below.

Remember that the ending of a story needs to leave an impression on the reader.

a) A story about a spaceship that crashes on an alien planet.

....

....

b) A story set on a desert island.

....

....

Writing Stories

Time to put all that short practice... into practice. Here are some exam-style questions to sink your teeth into.

 Q4 Answer the exam-style question below.

> You want to submit a piece of creative writing to be published in your local newspaper. The paper's editor will decide which submissions to publish.
>
> Write a short story that is set in your local area.

 Q5 Answer the exam-style question below.

> You are going to enter a writing competition at your local zoo. Your entry will be judged by a panel of people your age.
>
> Write the ending of a story about a penguin.

 Q6 Answer the exam-style question below.

> You are going to submit a story to an anthology aimed at people who have an interest in travel.
>
> Write a short story suggested by this picture:
>
>

Are you sitting comfortably? Then I'll begin...

Don't underestimate paper 1, question 5 — it's tempting to think it's less important than questions 1-4, but it's worth as many marks as all of the reading questions put together. Use your imagination to write something that really stands out.

Writing Descriptions

Q1 Write a description to match each of the following requirements.

    a) Use personification to describe an old car.

....

    b) Use a metaphor to describe an urban landscape.

....

    c) Use a simile to describe the feeling of embarrassment.

....

Q2 Write a descriptive sentence about a busy leisure centre based on each of the following senses.

    a) sight

....

    b) sound

....

    c) touch

....

    d) smell and / or taste

....

Q3 You have been asked to write a description of a family member. In the box below, draw a spider diagram showing your ideas for things you might include.

You could include some of the techniques on this page.

Writing Descriptions

Don't close your descriptive language bag o' tricks yet... these exam-style questions are just waiting to be lit up by your vocabulary. Have a go, then tick a box at the bottom of the page to show how you got on.

Q4 Answer the exam-style question below.

> You have a penpal of a similar age to you who lives in another country. In their last letter, they asked you to tell them about any interesting buildings in your area.
>
> Write a letter back to them in which you give a description of an interesting building.

Q5 Answer the exam-style question below.

> You are going to enter a writing competition run by your school newspaper. The competition is being judged by your head teacher.
>
> Write a description suggested by this picture:

Describe and conquer — that doesn't sound quite right somehow...

For a really interesting, vivid description, you need to <u>show</u> the reader what's going on instead of just <u>telling</u> them. E.g. instead of writing "Ajay was excited", you could write: "Ajay's eyes were bright, and his stance was upright and eager."

Writing Newspaper Articles

Q1 Read the exam question and then answer the questions below.

> "Students should be allowed time off for all religious holidays, not just Christmas and Easter."
> Write an article for your school newspaper giving your point of view on this statement.

a) What is the purpose and who are the audience in this question?

Purpose: .... **Audience:** ....

b) Write a rhetorical question which you could use in this article.

....

c) Make up a believable fact or statistic which you could include.

....

d) Write a short sentence for your article which contains some emotive language.

....

Q2 Read the question below, then write a good opening sentence on the lines underneath.

> "The human race is not doing enough to protect the planet's endangered species."
> Write a broadsheet newspaper article explaining your point of view on this statement.

....

....

Q3 Read the sentences below, then rewrite them so that they're suitable for an opinion column in a broadsheet newspaper.

Remember — opinion columns are generally written in a personal tone.

a) "Doctors have warned of the problems the nation faces if the number of smokers in this country does not decrease."

No-one likes being lectured, but the doctors' warnings are clear — we can't carry on like this.

b) "The government have today announced a policy that will see unsupervised children banned from public places."

....

c) "Temperatures soared across the country this weekend in an unprecedented heat wave."

....

Writing Newspaper Articles

 Q4 Read the following extract from a broadsheet newspaper article.

CRISIS FOR CLASSICAL MUSIC

A report released today by the RBMS (Royal British Music Society) claims that up to 50% of young people in Britain have never listened to a piece of classical music. A further 24% say that they have heard a piece of classical music, but 'would not choose' to listen to the genre.

The report, which was commissioned by the Society in response to a decline in attendance at many live concerts, has provoked concern amongst the musical fraternity, with many claiming that classical music could meet an untimely end if further action is not taken.

Luigi Piccolo, head of the world-renowned Royston Philharmonic Orchestra, said: "Over the next fifty years or so, we're going to become completely irrelevant. It's time to start appealing to a wider audience."

Write an opinion column to be published alongside this article, in which you explain your point of view on the report.

 Q5 Answer the exam-style question below.

> "Active hobbies, such as sports, are falling by the wayside because of the popularity of tablets and smartphones. Being constantly glued to screens is bad for our nation's health."
>
> Write an article for a broadsheet newspaper advising people to spend less time in front of screens and more time engaging in active hobbies.

 Q6 Answer the exam-style question below.

> "Going on a big holiday every year is a waste of money. People should make the most of the life they have at home instead of trying to find excitement elsewhere."
>
> Write an article for a broadsheet newspaper in which you argue the case for or against this statement.

I fell asleep whilst reading that — must have been a snooze-paper...

Hopefully you're now feeling suitably in-the-know about writing newspaper articles. Don't forget that there are different types of newspaper writing, though — read the question carefully, and adapt your tone, language and style to match.

    Section Four — Writing — Creative and Non-Fiction

Writing Leaflets and Travel Writing

Q1   Use the words in the box to complete the following sentences about travel writing.

opinions   conversational   newspapers   place   first   entertain

Travel writing is always about a specific .... It is commonly found in

.... and books. It is used to convey the writer's .... about

a place. Its purpose is often to .... It uses a .... tone

and is often written in the .... person in order to engage its audience.

Q2   Read the text below.

> Come to Caleb's Kitchen today, for:
> * Delicious, freshly made food.
> * A warm and welcoming environment.
> * And on top of all that, unbelievably low prices!

Caleb's plan to make the restaurant warm had backfired slightly.

a) Do you think this extract is from a leaflet or a piece of travel writing?

....

b) Write down a reason for your answer.

....

Q3   Read the exam-style question below, then write a suitable opening on the dotted lines.

> "Fast-food chains make it difficult for independent restaurants to make any money. They should be banned."
>
> Write the text for a leaflet to be distributed in your local area, in which you persuade the audience to agree with your point of view on this statement.

....

....

....

....

Writing Leaflets and Travel Writing

You'll know what's coming by now... yep, it's some exam-style questions to really test your talents.

 Q4 Read the following extract from a piece of travel writing.

> **Having decided we couldn't afford a holiday abroad this summer, my family found ourselves in a conundrum.** Just a few weeks into the school summer holidays, we were already sick of visiting the same old places, and with another month ahead of us, we decided to take action. After some research online, we eventually discovered Oakfall Island, a small island just a few miles out from the coastal town where we live.
>
> As it turns out, Oakfall Island is the perfect destination for a low-budget 'staycation'. We knew we were on to a winner when the kids loved the boat ride over from the mainland! The island itself did not disappoint — our campsite was fully equipped with clean shower blocks, a barbecue area and an adventure playground, and there were acres of open fields and forest for the kids to explore.
>
> With its ancient ruins and rolling hills, Oakfall Island is a relaxing escape from urban life that has something for everyone; my wife and I enjoyed our stay almost as much as the kids did. My wife loved exploring the small but perfectly formed local museum, and I found a reasonably priced restaurant that served the most delightful desserts I have ever tasted, as well as a small deli selling organic local produce.

Using details from this text, write the text for a leaflet in which you persuade the reader to visit Oakfall Island.

 Q5 Answer the exam-style question below.

> Your friend has said, "Learning a foreign language at school is pointless. You never get to use it outside the classroom, and you forget it as soon as you leave school."
>
> Write the text for a leaflet in which you advise students choosing their GCSE options to study a foreign language.

 Q6 Answer the exam-style question below.

> "Young people should widen their horizons. It's important that they travel and experience new cultures before they start their adult life."
>
> Write a piece of travel writing in which you explain your point of view on this statement.

Finished these? Travel write on over to the next page...

There's a lot going on in these pages. These types of writing could pop up in that pesky exam, though, so you need to make sure you've got your head around the styles and techniques of both of them before you move on to the next page.

     Section Four — Writing — Creative and Non-Fiction

Writing Reports, Essays and Reviews

Q1   Read the extracts below. Draw lines to match each one to the correct form.

a)

In summary, the red-tailed bat does not appear to be at immediate risk of extinction. However, in light of its ineffectual breeding habits, it merits close monitoring by conservationists.

Report

b)

All in all, the exhibition was a remarkably charming insight into the fascinating world of the red-tailed bat. If you happen to have a spare hour or two this weekend, I'd say it's more than worth the £15 entry fee.

Review

Q2   Each of the extracts below is inappropriate for a report.
Rewrite each one so that it's appropriate for this form.

a) "Some people agree with the idea of scrapping university fees, and some don't, so I'm not really sure what we should do."

....

....

b) "The whole idea's complete twaddle, to be honest."

....

c) "I really think we should invest in the new community centre!"

....

Q3   Read the question below, then write a brief plan to show how you would structure your answer.

"Space travel is expensive and dangerous. We should stop exploring space."
Write an essay in which you explain your point of view on this statement.

Introduction: ....

1) ....

2) ....

3) ....

Conclusion: ....

Writing Reports, Essays and Reviews

 Q4 Read the letter below, written by a local resident to their MP.

> *Dear Mr Yates,*
>
> *I write in order to urge you to take action on a fundamental matter. The glottalbug population in Brueton is rapidly declining, and we simply must take steps to stop this before irreparable damage is done to our local environment.*
>
> *Glottalbugs are very important to our village's ecosystem: we need them to pollinate our crops, which is crucial in our agricultural community. Many jobs in the area are reliant on a good harvest; without the glottalbug, unemployment rates will soar.*
>
> *Unfortunately, the scale of the operation required to rescue our six-legged friends is a large one, and it's rather expensive. We will need support from the council to be able to fix this problem. Please help the glottalbugs, Mr Yates; you are their last chance.*
>
> *Yours sincerely,*
>
> *Mr D. Range.*

Imagine you are Mr Yates. Write an essay to be posted on your local council's website, in which you explain your opinion on the problem.

 Q5 Answer the exam-style question below.

> "Footballers today make far too much money. They should be legally required to donate at least 50% of their earnings to charity."
>
> Write a report for the government on the benefits and drawbacks of this idea to advise them on whether or not it should be put into action.

 Q6 Answer the exam-style question below.

> Imagine you have just been to see a film.
>
> Write a review for your cinema's newsletter, in which you persuade your audience to go and see the film too.

I've reviewed the situation, and I think it's time for another biscuit...

It's worth trying to answer some of these questions as if you were in an exam. Time yourself, and make sure there's nothing around to distract you. It's tough, but it'll pay off in the long run — you won't have a lot of time on the day.

   Section Four — Writing — Creative and Non-Fiction

Writing Speeches

Q1 Read the following bits of advice for speech writing and circle if they're true (T) or false (F).

a) Speeches should start with a dramatic statement and then slowly wind down.   (T / F)

b) You should try to make your speech appropriate for reading out loud.   (T / F)

c) If you're writing a speech, it can be helpful to address your audience directly.   (T / F)

"Well helloooo Wembley!"

Q2 You are writing a speech to encourage local residents to recycle more often. Write a sentence for the speech which uses each of the following language techniques.

a) Directly addressing the audience

Sometimes the effort of sorting out your recycling feels like a big waste of your time.

b) A rhetorical question

....

c) An exclamation

....

d) A list of three

....

Ladies and Gentlemen, I declare that the time is right for some exam-style practice.

Q3 Answer the following exam-style question.

> "Pizza is too unhealthy. We should ban it from being served to anyone under the age of eighteen."
>
> Write a speech to be delivered at a national conference of restaurant-owners in which you argue your point of view on this statement.

I'm making an easy Italian meal for dinner — it's a pizza cake...

The questions on this page should have made you feel more confident about writing speeches that have a strong impact on their audience. Try to make your speech memorable — you really need to be able to engage your audience here.

Writing Letters

Q1 Look at the exam-style question below, then fill in the table to give the purpose, audience and register of the letter.

> Write a letter to your local council, in which you argue that there should be more facilities for teenagers in your local area.

Purpose	
Audience	
Register	(formal / informal)

Q2 How would you start and end letters to the following people? The first one has been done for you.

a) Your headteacher

Start: *Dear Ms Coombes* .... End: ....

b) Your best friend

Start: .... End: ....

c) Your local fire safety officer (you don't know their name)

Start: .... End: ....

Q3 Imagine you're writing a letter to your head of year to argue that year 11 should be provided with a common room. Write a short paragraph from this letter on the lines below.

....

....

....

....

One bit of exam practice stands between you and the end of section four — see it done and freedom is yours.

Q4 Answer the following exam-style question.

> "We should build more houses in rural areas. Having beautiful scenery is not as important as having a plentiful supply of housing for a growing population."
>
> Write a letter to a local newspaper editor explaining your point of view on this statement.

I'm quite good at writing letters — A, Q, R, Z, F...

Don't worry if you get a question that asks you to write in a more modern form, like an email. Just make sure you adapt your writing to the audience and purpose in the question, and definitely avoid including any text speak or smiley faces.

       Section Four — Writing — Creative and Non-Fiction

Paper 1 — Questions

In this section, you get to be the examiner. You'll look at some students' answers to exam questions and decide what marks they should get. It'll help you understand what the examiners are looking for — which will improve the quality of your answers. Here's how it works:

1) Read the sample exam questions and text on pages 62-65. They're similar in style to the ones you'll get in paper 1 (called Explorations in Creative Reading and Writing).

2) You don't have to answer the questions. Instead, on pages 66-75 there are some sample student answers for you to mark.

3) For each question, we've given you a mark scheme. You can use this to decide how many marks each of the sample answers is worth.

Section A — Reading

0 1   Read again the first part of the source, **lines 1 to 8**.

List **four** things from this part of the text about the child.

[4 marks]

0 2   Look in detail at **lines 9 to 23** of the source.

How does the writer use language here to describe the summer evening?

You could include the writer's choice of:

- words and phrases
- language features and techniques
- sentence forms.

[8 marks]

0 3   You now need to think about the **whole** of the **source**.

This text is from the opening of a short story.

How has the writer structured the text to interest you as a reader?

You could write about:

- what the writer focuses your attention on at the beginning
- how and why the writer changes this focus as the source develops
- any other structural features that interest you.

[8 marks]

Paper 1 — Questions

0 4 Focus this part of your answer on the second half
of the source, **from line 48 to the end**.

A student, having read this section of the text said: "The writer is successful
in showing the reader how both main characters are feeling, and he does
this in a variety of ways."

To what extent do you agree?

In your response, you could:

- write about your own impressions of how the characters are feeling
- evaluate how the writer has created these impressions
- support your opinions with references to the text.

[20 marks]

Section B — Writing

0 5 You have been chosen to represent your school at a national creative writing contest.

Your entry will be judged by a panel of teachers.

Either:

Write a description suggested by this picture:

Or:

Write the closing part of a story that takes place on a summer evening.

(24 marks for content and organisation
16 marks for technical accuracy)

[40 marks]

Paper 1 — Exam Source

This is the text to go with the questions on pages 62-63. It's the opening of a short story by Ray Bradbury, written in 1946. The story, set in 1927, is about a young boy living in a small town in the USA.

The Night

You are a child in a small town. You are, to be exact, eight years old, and it is growing late at night. Late for you, accustomed to bedding in at nine or nine-thirty: once in a while perhaps begging Mom or Dad to let you stay up later to hear Sam and Henry on that strange radio that is popular in this year of 1927. But most of the time you are in bed and snug at this time of night.

5   It is a warm summer evening. You live in a small house on a small street in the outer part of town where there are few street lights. There is only one store open, about a block away: Mrs Singer's. In the hot evening Mother has been ironing the Monday wash and you have been intermittently begging for ice cream and staring into the dark.

You and your mother are all alone at home in the warm darkness of summer. Finally, just before it
10   is time for Mrs Singer to close her store, Mother relents and tells you:
'Run get a pint of ice cream and be sure she packs it tight.'
You ask if you can get a scoop of chocolate ice cream on top, because you don't like vanilla, and Mother agrees. You clutch the money and run barefooted over the warm evening cement sidewalk, under the apple trees and oak trees, toward the store. The town is so quiet and far off, you can only
15   hear the crickets sounding in the spaces beyond the hot indigo trees that hold back the stars.

Your bare feet slap the pavement, you cross the street and find Mrs Singer moving ponderously about her store, singing Yiddish* melodies.
'Pint ice cream?' she says. 'Chocolate on top? Yes!'
You watch her fumble the metal top off the ice-cream freezer and manipulate the scoop, packing
20   the cardboard pint chock full with 'chocolate on top, yes!' You give the money, receive the chill, icy pack, and rubbing it across your brow and cheek, laughing, you thump barefootedly homeward. Behind you, the lights of the lonely little store blink out and there is only a street light shimmering on the corner, and the whole city seems to be going to sleep ...

Opening the screen door you find Mom still ironing. She looks hot and irritated, but she smiles just
25   the same.
'When will Dad be home from lodge-meeting?' you ask.
'About eleven-thirty or twelve,' Mother replies. She takes the ice cream to the kitchen, divides it. Giving you your special portion of chocolate, she dishes out some for herself and the rest is put away. 'For Skipper and your father when they come.'
30   Skipper is your brother. He is your older brother. He's twelve and healthy, red-faced, hawk-nosed, tawny-haired, broad-shouldered for his years, and always running. He is allowed to stay up later than you. Not much later, but enough to make him feel it is worthwhile having been born first. He is over on the other side of town this evening to a game of kick-the-can and will be home soon. He and the kids have been yelling, kicking, running for hours, having fun. Soon he will come clomping in,
35   smelling of sweat and green grass on his knees where he fell, and smelling very much in all ways like Skipper; which is natural.

You sit enjoying the ice cream. You are at the core of the deep quiet summer night. Your mother and yourself and the night all around this small house on this small street. You lick each spoon of ice cream thoroughly before digging for another, and Mom puts her ironing board away and the hot iron
40   in its case, and she sits in the armchair by the phonograph**, eating her dessert and saying, 'My lands, it was a hot day today. It's still hot. Earth soaks up all the heat and lets it out at night. It'll be soggy sleeping.'

You both sit there listening to the summer silence. The dark is pressed down by every window and door, there is no sound because the radio needs a new battery, and you have played all the
45   Knickerbocker Quartet records and Al Jolson and Two Black Crows records*** to exhaustion: so you just sit on the hardwood floor by the door and look out into the dark dark dark, pressing your nose against the screen until the flesh of its tip is molded into small dark squares.

Paper 1 — Exam Source

'I wonder where your brother is?' Mother says after a while. Her spoon scrapes on the dish. 'He should be home by now. It's almost nine-thirty.'

50   'He'll be here,' you say, knowing very well that he will be.

You follow Mom out to wash the dishes. Each sound, each rattle of spoon or dish is amplified in the baked evening. Silently, you go to the living room, remove the couch cushions and, together, yank it open and extend it down into the double bed that it secretly is. Mother makes the bed, punching pillows neatly to flump them up for your head. Then, as you are unbuttoning your shirt, she says:

55   'Wait awhile, Doug.'

'Why?'

'Because. I say so.'

'You look funny, Mom.'

Mom sits down a moment, then stands up, goes to the door, and calls. You listen to her calling and

60 calling Skipper. Skipper, Skiiiiiiiiiperrrrrrrr over and over. Her calling goes out into the summer warm dark and never comes back. The echoes pay no attention.

Skipper, Skipper, Skipper.

Skipper!

And as you sit on the floor a coldness that is not ice cream and not winter, and not part of summer's

65 heat, goes through you. You notice Mom's eyes sliding, blinking; the way she stands undecided and is nervous. All of these things.

She opens the screen door. Stepping out into the night she walks down the steps and down the front sidewalk under the lilac bush. You listen to her moving feet.

She calls again. Silence.

70   She calls twice more. You sit in the room. Any moment now Skipper will reply, from down the long long narrow street:

'All right, Mom! All right, Mother! Hey!'

But he doesn't answer. And for two minutes you sit looking at the made-up bed, the silent radio, the silent phonograph, at the chandelier with its crystal bobbins gleaming quietly, at the rug with the

75 scarlet and purple curlicues**** on it. You stub your toe on the bed purposely to see if it hurts. It does.

Whining, the screen door opens, and Mother says:

'Come on, Shorts. We'll take a walk.'

Glossary

* Yiddish — a language spoken by some Jewish people.

** phonograph — an old-fashioned device used for playing music records (sometimes called a gramophone).

*** Knickerbocker Quartet, Al Jolson and Two Black Crows — famous entertainment acts in the 1920s.

**** curlicues — decorative curls or twists

Paper 1, Question 1 — Mark Scheme

This page gives you advice and a mark scheme for marking question 1 of the sample exam. Read this information and digest it. Then you'll be ready to mark the student answers on p.67.

Here's a reminder of question 1

0 1   Read again the first part of the source, **lines 1 to 8**.

     List **four** things from this part of the text about the child.

                                                      [4 marks]

Question 1 is about finding four facts

1) Question 1 tests the ability to <u>find</u> information or ideas in the text.

2) There are a maximum of <u>four marks</u> available. <u>One mark</u> is awarded for <u>each fact</u>.

3) The facts <u>must</u> come from the right <u>part</u> of the text (lines 1 to 8), and they must be <u>true</u>.

4) The facts must be about the <u>child</u> in the story (Doug).

5) Answers can either <u>quote</u> the text exactly or <u>paraphrase</u> it.

Mark Ranger, Mark Jones, Mark Smith, and Mark Forsyth were all delighted to be given to the GCSE student.

Look out for answers like these

Here are a list of facts that the answers <u>may</u> have included. The child:

• lives in a small town	• likes to listen to the radio
• is eight years old	• lives in a small house
• is usually in bed at nine or nine-thirty	• lives on a small street
• sometimes begs his parents to let him stay up late	• lives in the outer part of town
	• likes ice cream

> You should also give marks for any other true, relevant facts from the correct part of the text.

Paper 1, Question 1 — Sample Answers

Now it's your turn to be the examiner.

1) Make sure you've <u>read</u> the <u>advice</u> on page 66.

2) Use it to give each of these answers a <u>mark</u> out of 4.
   The first answer has already been marked for you.

3) <u>Explain</u> how you've decided on the marks in the lines below the answers.

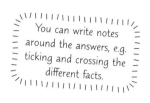

You can write notes around the answers, e.g. ticking and crossing the different facts.

Answer 1

0	1

1 *The child is "eight years old".*
2 *The child lives in the outer part of town.*
3 *The child is a boy.*
4 *The child usually goes to bed at nine or nine-thirty.*

This answer gets **3** mark(s) out of 4 because *1, 2 and 4 are facts about the child from the correct part of the text. 3 doesn't get a mark because we don't find out that the child is a boy until later in the text, when he's addressed as "Doug".*

Make sure you give reasons for your marking.

Answer 2

0	1

1 *The child is "to be exact, eight years old".*
2 *He is usually "bedding in at nine or nine-thirty".*
3 *The child lives in a small town.*
4 *His house is small too.*

This answer gets ☐ mark(s) out of 4 because ....
....
....

Answer 3

0	1

1 *The child lives on a small street.*
2 *He is alone with his mother in the house.*
3 *He is nine years old.*
4 *The child is scared of the dark.*

This answer gets ☐ mark(s) out of 4 because ....
....
....

Section Five — Sample Exams

Paper 1, Question 2 — Mark Scheme

It's time for question 2. Have a read of this page before marking the answers on page 69.

Here's question 2 again

| 0 | 2 |

Look in detail at **lines 9 to 23** of the source.

How does the writer use language here to describe the summer evening?

You could include the writer's choice of:

- words and phrases
- language features and techniques
- sentence forms.

[8 marks]

Question 2 is about analysing key language features

1) In question 2, answers need to explain how the writer has used language to achieve <u>effects</u> and <u>influence</u> the reader.

2) There are a maximum of <u>eight marks</u> available.

3) Points and examples need to come from the correct <u>part</u> of the text (lines 9 to 23).

4) The points all need to be about how the writer is describing the <u>summer evening</u>.

5) Answers should use the correct <u>technical terms</u> to identify different language features.

6) They then need to fully <u>explain</u> the effect that each language feature has on the reader.

Use this mark scheme to mark question 2

When you're marking an answer, look at this table and work out which <u>level description</u> fits the answer best, then award the answer the <u>mark</u> you think it deserves from that level.

Number of marks	What's written	How it's written
7-8 marks Level 4	In-depth and insightful analysis of the effects of a variety of language features.	Sophisticated technical terminology is used accurately. A perceptive selection of quotes are used to support points throughout.
5-6 marks Level 3	The effects of a selection of relevant language features are all clearly explained.	Technical terminology is used accurately throughout the answer. A variety of suitable quotes are used to support points throughout.
3-4 marks Level 2	Some language features are identified and their effects commented on.	Some technical terminology is used. Might not always be accurate. Some relevant quotes are used to support some of the points.
1-2 marks Level 1	Limited understanding of language features, with occasional comment.	Simple or no mention of subject terminology. May be inaccurate. Few points are supported by relevant quotations or references.

Paper 1, Question 2 — Sample Answers

It's time to be the examiner. Yippee.

1) Make sure you've <u>read</u> the <u>advice</u> and <u>mark scheme</u> on page 68.
2) Use them to give each of these answers a <u>mark</u> out of 8.
3) <u>Explain</u> how you've decided on the marks in the lines below the answers.

Answer 1

`0` `2`

    The writer uses the phrase "warm darkness", which tells the reader that the weather is hot and it's night-time. The writer repeats the word "warm" later to emphasise that this is important.
    The writer also uses onomatopoeia. For example, he uses words like "slap" and "thump". This helps the reader to imagine what that sounds like. The child wouldn't run without shoes on if it was cold, so the evening is hot. You can hear crickets, which appear when it is hot, so that also describes the summer evening.

This answer gets [ ] marks out of 8 because ....

....

....

....

....

Answer 2

`0` `2`

    In this part of the text, the writer suggests that the summer evening is calm by linking it to the idea of sleep. For example, the light imagery in the phrase "lights of the lonely little store blink out" is like turning a light off before going to bed. The phrase "the whole city seems to be going to sleep" supports this.
    The writer adds to this sense of calm by describing the evening as quiet. "The town is so quiet" that you can "only hear the crickets". This means that the "slap" and "thump" of the child's feet are amplified, as if he's disturbing the stillness; the writer uses onomatopoeia here to emphasise this disturbance to the reader.
    The writer also highlights the heat of the evening. The repetition of the word "warm" suggests that this is a significant part of the evening's atmosphere. This is then contrasted with the "icy pack" that the child rubs across his face — the writer is describing a contrasting sensation to emphasise the evening's overall heat.

This answer gets [ ] marks out of 8 because ....

....

....

....

....

Paper 1, Question 3 — Mark Scheme

Question 3 is another 8 mark question. Make sure you're clear on this page before you dive into page 71.

This is what question 3 looks like

| 0 | 3 |

You now need to think about the **whole** of the **source**.

This text is from the opening of a short story.

How has the writer structured the text to interest you as a reader?

You could write about:

- what the writer focuses your attention on at the beginning
- how and why the writer changes this focus as the source develops
- any other structural features that interest you.

[8 marks]

Question 3 is about the structure of the whole text

1) Question 3 is about how the writer has used structure to achieve <u>effects</u> and <u>influence</u> the reader.

2) There are a maximum of <u>eight marks</u> available.

3) Points and examples can come from <u>any</u> part of the text.

4) Because this question is about <u>all</u> of the text, answers will need to talk about its <u>overall structure</u>.

5) However, good answers will also comment on a <u>range</u> of other structural features, including:

- <u>Paragraph-level</u> features, e.g. <u>connections</u> between paragraphs, <u>shifts</u> in perspective or topic <u>repetition</u>.

- <u>Sentence-level</u> features, e.g. how the <u>position</u> of certain sentences within a text creates interest and affects its <u>overall structure</u>.

Here is a mark scheme for question 3

The table below describes what an answer needs to be like for each <u>level</u>.

Number of marks	What's written	How it's written
7-8 marks Level 4	Analyses the effects of a range of structural features confidently and in detail.	Sophisticated technical terminology is used accurately. Uses a perceptive range of examples from across the source.
5-6 marks Level 3	The effects of a variety of structural features are clearly explained.	Technical terminology is used accurately throughout. Suitable examples from the whole text are used and explained.
3-4 marks Level 2	The effects of some structural features are explained.	Some technical terminology is used. May not always be accurate. Some points are supported with relevant examples from the text.
1-2 marks Level 1	Basic attempts to comment on a few structural features in a simple manner.	Simple or no mention of subject terminology. May be inaccurate. Few references are made to the text and are not always relevant.

Paper 1, Question 3 — Sample Answers

Here's another pair of answers for you to assess.

1) Make sure you've <u>read</u> the <u>advice</u> and <u>mark scheme</u> on page 70.

2) Use them to give each of these answers a <u>mark</u> out of 8.

3) <u>Explain</u> how you've decided on the marks in the lines below the answers.

Answer 1

| 0 | 3 |

The text is structured to interest the reader by progressing them from a state of relative calm to a commotion of nervous energy. The opening of the extract — "You are a child in a small town" — instantly creates a sense of normality; this could be any child in any small town, anywhere in the world. In its relatability, this simple beginning establishes an atmosphere of tranquillity.

As the text progresses, the writer draws the reader into the child's world by introducing a period of childish excitement. The speech "Run get a pint of ice cream", beginning with an imperative verb, creates a sense of action, which signals a brief passage of lively activity before returning to the calm and contentment of the early part of the text.

The text then changes more significantly in line 54, indicated by the connective "Then", which highlights that something important is about to occur. From this point, the tone of the extract becomes more tense, with shorter sentences used to emphasise the growing concern over Skipper's absence. This change in tone is important because it encourages the reader to feel worried about Skipper's whereabouts.

This answer gets ☐ marks out of 8 because ....

....

....

....

....

Answer 2

| 0 | 3 |

To start with there are lots of calm statements, like "It is a warm summer evening" and "you are a child". Then the writer uses excited speech as the child buys ice cream. After that, the text becomes calm again when the writer talks about Skipper. Towards the end, the writer uses tension as the mother calls to Skipper. At the end, the tension goes a bit and they decide to "take a walk."

This answer gets ☐ marks out of 8 because ....

....

....

....

....

Paper 1, Question 4 — Mark Scheme

This is the last question in Section A, but it's worth a huge 20 marks, so read this page carefully.

Here's question 4 to refresh your memory

0 4   Focus this part of your answer on the second half
of the source, **from line 48 to the end**.

A student, having read this section of the text said: "The writer
is successful in showing the reader how both main characters
are feeling, and he does this in a variety of ways."

To what extent do you agree?

In your response, you could:

• write about your own impressions of how the characters are feeling
• evaluate how the writer has created these impressions
• support your opinions with references to the text.

[20 marks]

Question 4 is about giving your own opinion

1)   Question 4 tests the ability to <u>evaluate</u> a text, and to explain
your personal <u>opinion</u> on a statement about it.

2)   This opinion needs to be supported with <u>examples</u> from the text,
with an explanation of <u>how</u> each example supports the opinion.

3)   Points and examples need to come from the correct <u>part</u> of the text (line 48 to the end).

4)   Answers need to discuss <u>both</u> of the main characters — Doug <u>and</u> his mother.

5)   There are a maximum of <u>twenty marks</u> available for this question.

This is the mark scheme for question 4

This table will help you to assess the answers on the next page.

Number of marks	What's written	How it's written
16-20 marks Level 4	In-depth, personal response to the statement, with critical, detailed analysis of writer's choices.	Opinions are convincingly explained and fully supported with relevant, useful quotations.
11-15 marks Level 3	Clearly explained response to the statement that discusses the effect of the writer's choices.	Opinions are clearly expressed and mostly supported with appropriate quotations.
6-10 marks Level 2	An attempt at a personal response to the statement; some comments on the effect of writer's methods.	Some opinions are explained and supported with quotations or examples.
1-5 marks Level 1	Limited response to the statement, with little mention of the effect of the writer's methods.	Only a few opinions are supported with relevant quotations or examples.

Paper 1, Question 4 — Sample Answers

Here are two <u>extracts</u> from responses to question 4 for you to mark.

1) Make sure you've <u>read</u> the <u>advice</u> and <u>mark scheme</u> on page 72.
2) Use them to give each of these answers a <u>mark</u> out of 20.
3) <u>Explain</u> how you've decided on the marks in the lines below the answers.

The sample answers here are just extracts. The ones you write in the exam will need to be longer — but you should still mark these out of 20.

Answer 1

`0 4`

    I agree with the student, because the writer is successful in showing me how the young boy (Doug) is feeling. One of the ways in which the writer does this is using the second person to address the reader — this puts me in Doug's position, showing me his perspective in phrases like "knowing very well that he will be". Seeing things through Doug's eyes helps me to see his confidence in his brother.

    I also agree with the student because I know how the mother is feeling. The writer describes her as "undecided" and "nervous" to make the reader see that she's feeling panicked. In addition, the writer uses an image of her "eyes sliding, blinking" to help me to imagine how worried she must be about her eldest son.

This answer gets [ ] marks out of 20 because ....
....
....
....
....

Answer 2

`0 4`

    I think the student is right to say that the writer is successful in showing us how Doug is feeling, because his point of view is the perspective of the narrative. However, I don't know if I really understand the mother.

    Doug's feelings are obvious in the text. The writer uses the present tense — phrases like "You listen" and "You notice" to guide the reader's senses as if they were Doug's. When Doug deliberately stubs his toe on the bed and it hurts, I feel like I know how that feels, and I worry about Skipper too.

    But I don't know if I can understand the mother, because she's more separate. When she says "Because. I say so." she doesn't give her real reasons. She doesn't explain why they're going to take a walk either, just using a short sentence instead.

This answer gets [ ] marks out of 20 because ....
....
....
....
....

Paper 1, Question 5 — Mark Scheme

This question is worth 40 marks — it's a bit of a whopper. Make sure you know how to mark it.

Here's a quick recap of question 5

0 5 You have been chosen to represent your school at a national creative writing contest.

Your entry will be judged by a panel of teachers.

Either:

Write a description suggested by this picture:

Or:

Write the closing part of a story that takes place on a summer evening.

(24 marks for content and organisation
16 marks for technical accuracy)

[40 marks]

Look at this mark scheme for question 5

1) Question 5 tests <u>two</u> things. There are 24 marks for having an <u>interesting</u> and <u>well-organised</u> answer, and 16 marks for good <u>technical accuracy</u>, including <u>spelling</u>, <u>punctuation</u> and <u>grammar</u>.

2) The best answers also need to be really well-matched to the <u>form</u>, <u>purpose</u> and <u>audience</u> that are specified in the question.

	Content and organisation		Technical accuracy
19-24 marks Level 4	Imaginative use of structure and language techniques, thoroughly matched to form, purpose and audience.	13-16 marks Level 4	Ambitious use of vocabulary; confidently uses a wide range of grammar and punctuation.
13-18 marks Level 3	Effective writing, using a clear structure and language techniques. Matched to form, purpose and audience.	9-12 marks Level 3	Largely suitable, varied vocabulary; a range of mostly correct grammar and punctuation.
7-12 marks Level 2	Mostly matched to form, purpose and audience. Some language techniques and structural features.	5-8 marks Level 2	Attempts a variety of vocabulary, punctuation and grammar, sometimes successfully.
1-6 marks Level 1	Some sense of purpose, a few relevant ideas linked together, a mostly disorganised structure.	1-4 marks Level 1	Simple vocabulary, grammar and punctuation are used with inaccuracies throughout.

Paper 1, Question 5 — Sample Answers

Here are two sample answers to the first task in question 5 — a <u>description</u> suggested by the picture.

1) Make sure you've <u>read</u> the <u>mark scheme</u> on page 74.

2) Mark each criteria <u>separately</u>, then <u>add</u> up the two marks to get a total out of 40.

3) <u>Explain</u> how you've decided on the marks in the lines below the answers.

These answers are only <u>extracts</u> — your exam answers will need to be much longer than this.

Answer 1

| 0 | 5 |

The street was empty except for one figure: it was a little boy. He was roughly dressed. His shoelaces were untied or missing. His hair was as messy as a bird's nest. The little boy's T-shirt was lime green with darker green grass stanes.

He stood out in the street. The houses were organised as neatly as a box of matchsticks. Some of the lawns had flowers — like roses and sunflowers.

It was a warm, hot evening, just turning dark but with a bit of light. It shone on the boy like an old-fashioned lantern. It lit his face like a torch. There were no clouds and no stars. Just the little boy, alone in the street, all by himself.

Content and organisation = [ ] / 24 ....

Technical accuracy = [ ] / 16 ....

Total = [ ] / 40 ....

Answer 2

| 0 | 5 |

The sun sets slowly on oak Street; it clings to the branches of the trees, reluctant to leave. The branches shuffle in its half-light, dappling the pathways below with kaleidoscopic patterns of yellow, orange, black, yellow again. Outside number 42, a cat tries to catch the colours.

A child walks slowly down oak Street. He pauses to watch the determined tabby playing in the light, stretches out his arm beneath the tree so it, too, is speckled with the rays. The cat is disturbed by the intrusion and, affronted, skulks off to hide.

The child ambles on. He strokes his fingers through hedges, punts pebbles along the path, tosses acorns into the air. When the trees end he squints in the brightness and shields his eyes as if in a salute. He wonders where the cat is.

Content and organisation = [ ] / 24 ....

Technical accuracy = [ ] / 16 ....

Total = [ ] / 40 ....

Section Five — Sample Exams

Paper 2 — Questions

It's time to be the examiner again. This time, the questions below are like the ones you'll see in paper 2 (called Writers' Viewpoints and Perspectives). You need to have a look at the sample answers to each of the exam questions, then decide what marks they deserve. Here's a reminder of how to do it:

1) Read the sample exam questions and the two source texts on pages 76-79. They're similar in style to the ones you'll get in paper 2 of your GCSE English Language exam.

2) Remember — you don't have to actually answer the questions.

3) Instead, on pages 80-89 there are some sample answers for you to mark, with some advice and mark schemes to help you along the way.

Why is this hot dog like paper 2 section A?
It uses two sauces...

Section A — Reading

0 1   Read again **source A**, from **lines 1 to 19**.

Choose **four** statements below which are TRUE.

- Shade the boxes of the ones that you think are true
- Choose a maximum of four statements.

A   Monica Albelli thinks being a nanny is a difficult job. ☐

B   Parents and children usually look for the same things in a nanny. ☐

C   Parents almost always agree on the duties of a nanny. ☐

D   Lesley and Brian are both professionals of a similar age. ☐

E   Lesley and Brian are affectionate parents. ☐

F   Brian likes his children to play educational games. ☐

G   Both parents think discipline is important. ☐

H   Lesley and Brian sometimes gave Monica conflicting instructions. ☐

[4 marks]

Paper 2 — Questions

0 2   You need to refer to **source A** and **source B** for this question.

Use details from **both** sources. Write a summary of
the differences between Lesley and Mrs Sidgwick.

[8 marks]

0 3   You now need to refer **only** to **source B**.

How does Charlotte Brontë use language to try to influence her sister?

[12 marks]

0 4   For this question you need to refer to the **whole** of **source A** together
with **source B**.

Compare how the two writers convey their different attitudes to
looking after other people's children.

In your answer, you could:

* compare their different attitudes
* compare the methods they use to convey their attitudes
* support your ideas with references to both texts.

[16 marks]

Section B — Writing

0 5   "In order to prepare young adults for the challenges of raising a family, it should
be made compulsory for them to spend time volunteering with young children."

Write a speech, to be given to your local council, in which
you argue your point of view on this statement.

(24 marks for content and organisation
16 marks for technical accuracy)

[40 marks]

Paper 2 — Exam Source A

The following text is an extract from an article written by a nanny, Monica Albelli.
It was published in a broadsheet newspaper in 2013.

Confessions of a Nanny

Being a nanny — whether you're a Mary Poppins, a Nanny McPhee or a Mrs Doubtfire — is a very tricky job. You have to be liked by two opposing "teams" to which a "perfect" nanny means completely different things. "You must be kind, you must be witty, very sweet and fairly pretty... If you don't scold and dominate us, we will never give you cause to hate us" — this is how the

5   children in Mary Poppins, Michael and Jane, want the newspaper ad for their nanny to read. Their father, Mr Banks, is keener on discipline. Mrs Banks seems to believe perfection lies somewhere in between that and the children's ideal.

I have always loved children and had a natural ability to connect with them with ease, no matter their gender, nationality or character. But when you're a nanny, kids come with parents.

10   And parents come with problems, opinions and expectations of their own, often in conflict between themselves.

Lesley, a successful publisher, and Brian, a dentist, were Scots in their mid-40s. They worked long hours but seemed to love Therese, seven, Tom, nine, and William, 11. Their approach when it came to the kids' upbringing though was completely different from each other. Confident

15   and motivated, Lesley believed her children's time should be spent doing homework, reading books or playing educational games. Brian, cheerful and laid back, wanted us to "just have fun". He asked me not to be strict with the kids, while Lesley kept pressuring me to turn them into responsible and hard-working individuals. I would arrive at their house to find a note from Brian, asking me to take them to the park, and then receive a text from Lesley with a to-do list.

20   Lesley would often come home late to find the kids already asleep. "I'm not a good mum," she once confessed. "I'm actually a bit jealous. I think they are starting to like you more than they like me."

I reassured her that this was not true and that she was doing her best.

The kids and I had bonded. Once, as I was getting ready to leave, Tom curled around my

25   leg, while Lesley tried to persuade him he had to let me go. They liked having me around so much that they started asking Brian if I could sleep over. Had we bonded too much?

Then things changed. Lesley seemed upset about something, and Brian was more and more absent. One day they told me they wouldn't be needing me any more as they had decided to get an au pair, who could also help with the house. I knew that wasn't the real reason. They had, I

30   realised, been asking me to become everything they weren't and, as soon as I started to achieve that, they felt threatened.

I tried to see it from their point of view. Being a nanny is difficult, but being a parent is even harder. Having a nanny is also hard.

I remembered what a friend used to say whenever I shared my frustrations with her: "You

35   care too much. It's just a job."

Should a nanny be indifferent, see herself as a doctor and treat all family members as her patients, being impartial and never getting emotionally involved? How can Mary Poppins be indifferent? She is cool and funny, strict at times, but always caring — the perfect nanny. But she is a fictional character, and so are Mr and Mrs Banks, and Michael and Jane.

40   Many dysfunctional families later, I have learned to care at the same time as keeping a distance, and that there is no such thing as the perfect family — or the perfect nanny.

Paper 2 — Exam Source B

The following text was written by Charlotte Brontë, a famous 19th-century author. Charlotte was working as a governess — a woman employed to teach and care for the children in a household. This is an extract from a letter written to her sister in 1839.

Dearest Lavinia,*

I am most exceedingly obliged to you for the trouble you have taken in seeking up my things and sending them all right. The box and its contents were most acceptable.

I have striven hard to be pleased with my new situation. The country, the house, and the
5 grounds are, as I have said, divine. But, alack-a-day! there is such a thing as seeing all beautiful around you — pleasant woods, winding white paths, green lawns, and blue sunshiny sky — and not having a free moment or a free thought left to enjoy them in. The children are constantly with me, and more riotous, perverse, unmanageable cubs never grew. As for correcting them, I soon quickly found that was entirely out of the question: they are to do as they like. A complaint to Mrs. Sidgwick
10 brings only black looks upon oneself, and unjust, partial excuses to screen the children. I have tried that plan once. It succeeded so notably that I shall try it no more. I said in my last letter that Mrs. Sidgwick did not know me. I now begin to find that she does not intend to know me, that she cares nothing in the world about me except to contrive how the greatest possible quantity of labour may be squeezed out of me, and to that end she overwhelms me with oceans of needlework, yards of cambric
15 to hem, muslin night-caps to make, and, above all things, dolls to dress. I do not think she likes me at all, because I can't help being shy in such an entirely novel scene, surrounded as I have hitherto been by strange and constantly changing faces. I see now more clearly than I have ever done before that a private governess has no existence, is not considered as a living and rational being except as connected with the wearisome duties she has to fulfil. While she is teaching the children, working for
20 them, amusing them, it is all right. If she steals a moment for herself she is a nuisance. Nevertheless, Mrs. Sidgwick is universally considered an amiable woman. Her manners are fussily affable. She talks a great deal, but as it seems to me not much to the purpose. Perhaps I may like her better after a while. At present I have no call to her. Mr. Sidgwick is in my opinion a hundred times better — less profession, less bustling condescension, but a far kinder heart.
25 As to Mrs. Collins' report that Mrs. Sidgwick intended to keep me permanently, I do not think that such was ever her design. Moreover, I would not stay without some alterations. For instance, this burden of sewing would have to be removed. It is too bad for anything. I never in my whole life had my time so fully taken up.

Don't show this letter to papa or aunt, only to Branwell.** They will think I am never satisfied
30 wherever I am. I complain to you because it is a relief, and really I have had some unexpected mortifications to put up with. However, things may mend, but Mrs. Sidgwick expects me to do things that I cannot do — to love her children and be entirely devoted to them. I am really very well. I am so sleepy that I can write no more. I must leave off. Love to all. — Good-bye.

C. BRONTË.

Glossary
* A nickname for Charlotte's sister, Emily.
** Branwell — their brother.

Paper 2, Question 1 — Mark Scheme

This page tells you what you should be looking for in the answers to paper 2, question 1.

Here's a reminder of question 1

| 0 | 1 | Read again **source A**, from **lines 1 to 19**.

Choose **four** statements below which are TRUE.

- Shade the boxes of the ones that you think are true
- Choose a maximum of four statements.

A   Monica Albelli thinks being a nanny is a difficult job. ☐

B   Parents and children usually look for the same things in a nanny. ☐

C   Parents almost always agree on the duties of a nanny. ☐

D   Lesley and Brian are both professionals of a similar age. ☐

E   Lesley and Brian are affectionate parents. ☐

F   Brian likes his children to play educational games. ☐

G   Both parents think discipline is important. ☐

H   Lesley and Brian sometimes gave Monica conflicting instructions. ☐

[4 marks]

Question 1 asks you to pick four true statements

1) Question 1 is looking for the ability to <u>find</u> information or ideas in the source text.

2) Only <u>four</u> of the statements are true. Answers need to select the <u>correct</u> four — one mark is awarded for <u>each</u> correct answer.

3) In this question, the <u>correct answers</u> are A, D, E and H.

Use the information on this page to mark the sample answers

1) On the next page there are three <u>sample answers</u> to this question.

2) Use the advice above to give each of these sample answers a <u>mark out of 4</u>.

3) Then <u>explain</u> how you've decided on the marks in the lines below the answers.

4) The <u>first</u> answer has already been marked for you.

Paper 2, Question 1 — Sample Answers

Answer 1

A   Monica Albelli thinks being a nanny is a difficult job.   ▓

B   Parents and children usually look for the same things in a nanny.   ▓

C   Parents almost always agree on the duties of a nanny.   ☐

D   Lesley and Brian are both professionals of a similar age.   ☐

E   Lesley and Brian are affectionate parents.   ▓

F   Brian likes his children to play educational games.   ☐

G   Both parents think discipline is important.   ▓

H   Lesley and Brian sometimes gave Monica conflicting instructions.   ☐

This answer gets ⟨2⟩ marks out of 4 because *A and E are facts that can be found in the text, but the student has also picked B and G, which contradict the text — the answer loses two marks because of this.*

Answer 2

A   Monica Albelli thinks being a nanny is a difficult job.   ▓

B   Parents and children usually look for the same things in a nanny.   ☐

C   Parents almost always agree on the duties of a nanny.   ▓

D   Lesley and Brian are both professionals of a similar age.   ▓

E   Lesley and Brian are affectionate parents.   ☐

F   Brian likes his children to play educational games.   ☐

G   Both parents think discipline is important.   ☐

H   Lesley and Brian sometimes gave Monica conflicting instructions.   ▓

This answer gets ⟨ ⟩ marks out of 4 because ....

....

Answer 3

A   Monica Albelli thinks being a nanny is a difficult job.   ▓

B   Parents and children usually look for the same things in a nanny.   ☐

C   Parents almost always agree on the duties of a nanny.   ☐

D   Lesley and Brian are both professionals of a similar age.   ☐

E   Lesley and Brian are affectionate parents.   ▓

F   Brian likes his children to play educational games.   ☐

G   Both parents think discipline is important.   ▓

H   Lesley and Brian sometimes gave Monica conflicting instructions.   ▓

This answer gets ⟨ ⟩ marks out of 4 because ....

....

Paper 2, Question 2 — Mark Scheme

It's time for question 2. Have a read of the info on this page, then try marking the answers on page 83.

Read question 2 to refresh your memory

| 0 | 2 | You need to refer to **source A** and **source B** for this question.

Use details from **both** sources. Write a summary of
the differences between Lesley and Mrs Sidgwick.

[8 marks]

Question 2 is about comparing two things

1) Question 2 tests the ability to <u>find</u> information in texts, then <u>summarise</u> the information clearly.

2) There are <u>eight marks</u> available.

3) Points and examples can come from <u>anywhere</u> in either text, but they need to be focused on the <u>characters</u> in the question — Lesley and Mrs Sidgwick.

4) Answers need to <u>summarise</u> the <u>differences</u> between Lesley and Mrs Sidgwick — this means making a <u>point</u> about the two characters, backing it up with <u>evidence</u>, then <u>explaining how</u> the quote shows that the two characters are <u>different</u>.

5) To get the best marks, answers need to <u>interpret</u> information from both texts. This might include thinking about them in a bit more depth, and picking out information that isn't <u>immediately obvious</u> to the reader.

Use this mark scheme for question 2

The table below describes what an answer needs to be like for each level. When you're marking an answer, look at this table and work out which <u>level description</u> fits the answer best, then award the answer the <u>mark</u> you think it deserves from that level.

Number of marks	What's written	How it's written
7-8 marks Level 4	An in-depth understanding of the differences between the characters.	Links the two texts in a perceptive way, including interpreting some implicit details. Chooses quotes and examples that fully support points.
5-6 marks Level 3	A good understanding of the differences between the characters	Makes connections between the two texts and starts to analyse them. Uses a range of relevant quotes to support points.
3-4 marks Level 2	Some differences between the characters are pointed out.	Some attempts to make inferences and link the two texts together. Some points are supported by relevant quotations.
1-2 marks Level 1	Mentions simple differences between the characters.	Paraphrases the texts and makes simple links between them. A few simple quotes or references are included.

Paper 2, Question 2 — Sample Answers

Pens at the ready — it's time to have a go at marking some answers.

1) Make sure you've <u>read</u> the <u>advice</u> and <u>mark scheme</u> on page 82.

2) Use them to give each of these answers a <u>mark</u> out of 8.

3) <u>Explain</u> how you've decided on the marks in the lines below the answers.

Answer 1

0	2

Mrs Sidgwick and Lesley have different approaches to raising children. Mrs Sidgwick thinks that her children should be allowed to "do as they like," but Lesley wants her children to become "responsible and hard-working individuals", so she sends Monica "a to-do list" of things they should do each day.

Also, Lesley and Mrs Sidgwick have different opinions on childcare. Mrs Sidgwick "expects" Charlotte to "love her children and be entirely devoted to them". Monica, on the other hand, becomes too close to Lesley's children, and then Lesley sacks her.

This answer gets [ ] marks out of 8 because ....

....

....

....

....

Answer 2

0	2

Mrs Sidgwick and Lesley are very different people, particularly in their attitude towards the people they employ. Mrs Sidgwick does not treat her governess as if she's a person; it is thanks to Mrs Sidgwick that Charlotte feels as if she is "not considered as a living and rational being". In contrast, Monica hints that, to an extent, Lesley treated her as a friend: for example, she "confessed" to Monica about her insecurities regarding her children.

Lesley seems to care more about other people's feelings than Mrs Sidgwick. Lesley doesn't tell Monica the "real reason" that she was fired, suggesting that she might be trying to save Monica's feelings. In contrast, Charlotte writes as if Mrs Sidgwick does not consider Charlotte's wellbeing; Charlotte has "never" been so "fully" occupied before, which makes her so tired that she "can write no more".

This answer gets [ ] marks out of 8 because ....

....

....

....

....

Paper 2, Question 3 — Mark Scheme

Have a look at the information on this page, which is all about how to mark paper 2, question 3.

Here's a reminder of question 3

| 0 | 3 |

You now need to refer **only** to **source B**.

How does Charlotte Brontë use language to try to influence her sister?

[12 marks]

Question 3 is about how one of the texts uses language

1) In question 3, answers need to explain how the writer has used language to achieve an <u>effect</u> on the reader (Charlotte Brontë's sister).

2) Points and examples <u>must</u> come from Source B, and they need to relate <u>specifically</u> to what the <u>question</u> is asking for, i.e. how language is used to <u>influence</u> Brontë's sister.

3) Answers could mention specific <u>words and phrases</u>, <u>language techniques</u> (such as metaphors and alliteration) and <u>sentence structures</u>.

4) There are <u>twelve marks</u> available for this question.

Julia used some 'interesting' words and phrases to express her feelings during the bungee jump.

Read this mark scheme for question 3

Use this table to mark the answers on the next page.

Number of marks	What's written	How it's written
10-12 marks Level 4	Sophisticated, in-depth analysis of the effect of a variety of language features.	A good variety of relevant technical terminology is used. Uses a range of interesting quotes that support points well.
7-9 marks Level 3	The effects of the writer's choice of language features are explained clearly.	Technical terms are used accurately throughout. Includes a range of quotes that are appropriate to the points made.
4-6 marks Level 2	Some comments on the effects of the writer's language choices.	Some technical terms are used, but not always correctly. Includes some suitable quotes, but may use some that aren't relevant.
1-3 marks Level 1	Simple comments that show a basic awareness of the effects of language.	Some technical terminology is referred to in a simple way. Makes some simple references to the text.

Paper 2, Question 3 — Sample Answers

Here's a pair of <u>extracts</u> from student answers for you to assess.

1) Make sure you've <u>read</u> the <u>advice</u> and <u>mark scheme</u> on page 84.

2) Use them to give each of these student answers a <u>mark</u> out of 12.

3) <u>Explain</u> how you've decided on the marks in the lines below the answers.

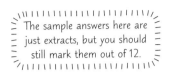
The sample answers here are just extracts, but you should still mark them out of 12.

Answer 1

| 0 | 3 |

_____Charlotte Brontë uses a metaphor: she says that Mrs Sidgwick gives her "oceans of needlework". She is comparing the jobs she is given to an ocean, which would help her sister understand that they're enormous.

_____Charlotte's work seems very overwhelming. She tells her sister that she has "no existence" apart from her "duties", and "can't help being shy". This descriptive language makes it seem like her job has taken over her life, so her sister might have felt sympathy for her when she read that.

This answer gets [　] marks out of 12 because ....

....

....

....

....

Answer 2

| 0 | 3 |

_____Brontë uses a combination of formal and informal language in order to influence her sister. She uses polite, formal language in places, such as the phrase "I am most exceedingly obliged"; this is a courtesy that would make her sister feel pleased. This formal language is then combined with familiar terms like "papa" and informal phrases, such as "Love to all" to appeal to the relationship between Brontë and her sister, which has the overall effect of making Brontë more likeable. This in turn would make her sister more inclined to agree with Brontë's viewpoint.

_____Brontë's language is also used to express her viewpoint in a strong and compelling way, which helps to influence her sister into sympathising with her difficulties. For example, she uses a list of adjectives, describing the children she takes care of as "riotous, perverse, unmanageable". The cumulative effect of these negative adjectives helps to emphasise Brontë's displeasure with her current situation, which encourages her sister to sympathise with her difficulties.

This answer gets [　] marks out of 12 because ....

....

....

....

....

Paper 2, Question 4 — Mark Scheme

Question 4 is the last question in section A, and it's worth a crucial 16 marks.

Have a read of question 4 to refresh your memory

0 4 For this question you need to refer to the **whole** of **source A** together with **source B**.

Compare how the two writers convey their different attitudes to looking after other people's children.

In your answer, you could:

- compare their different attitudes
- compare the methods they use to convey their attitudes
- support your ideas with references to both texts.

[16 marks]

Question 4 is about comparing the writers' attitudes

1) Question 4 tests the ability to compare <u>how</u> the writers express their <u>viewpoints</u>.

2) There are a maximum of <u>sixteen marks</u> available for this question.

3) Answers need to <u>identify</u> the writers' viewpoints, <u>support</u> these observations with <u>examples</u> from the text, and then explain <u>how</u> these examples convey the writers' points of view.

4) Answers also need to fully <u>develop</u> each point by making <u>links</u> between the texts and <u>comparing</u> the attitudes of <u>both</u> writers.

5) There are three <u>bullet points</u> at the end of this question. A good answer needs to include responses to <u>all three</u> of them.

Use this mark scheme to assess question 4

This table will help you to mark the answers on the next page.

Number of marks	What's written	How it's written
13-16 marks Level 4	A detailed, insightful comparison of the writers' attitudes, which demonstrates a perceptive understanding of the differences between the two viewpoints. In-depth analysis of the methods each writer uses to convey their point of view.	Points are consistently supported by precise quotations from both texts.
9-12 marks Level 3	The writers' attitudes are clearly compared, showing a clear understanding of the differences between the two viewpoints. Answer includes relevant discussion of the methods used to convey both writers' ideas.	A good range of appropriate quotations are used to support points.
5-8 marks Level 2	Some attempt to compare writers' attitudes, identifying some differences between their viewpoints and sometimes commenting on techniques used to convey them.	Includes a range of quotes, not always relevant.
1-4 marks Level 1	Basic identification 2 the two writers' attitudes and the differences between them, with only a limited awareness of the different ideas expressed in each text. Makes a few very simple references to methods used.	Some basic textual details or references, but many points are unsupported.

Paper 2, Question 4 — Sample Answers

Here are two <u>extracts</u> from student responses to question 4 for you.

1) Make sure you've <u>read</u> the <u>advice</u> and <u>mark scheme</u> on page 86.
2) Use them to give each of these student answers a <u>mark</u> out of 16.
3) <u>Explain</u> how you've decided on the marks in the lines below the answers.

Like in question 3, these answers are only extracts — your answers would need to be longer than these.

Answer 1

0	4

Both writers think that looking after children is hard — Brontë describes her job as a "burden" which suggests that it's hard. Monica Albelli calls being a nanny "tricky" and "difficult". However, the two writers are different about why they think it's hard. Brontë doesn't like being asked to "love" somebody else's children and she says she "cannot" do it. Albelli finds it hard not to bond "too much" with her children.

The writers are also different because Albelli likes looking after other people's children, but Brontë doesn't. She says it's "riotous". Albelli's friend says "You care too much", showing that Albelli does care about her work.

This answer gets ☐ marks out of 16 because ....
....
....
....
....

Answer 2

0	4

Brontë's letter suggests that she feels limited and confined by the duties involved in looking after other people's children. She refers to her wards as being "constantly" with her. Brontë's choice of adverb suggests that she gets no respite from the children; it also indicates that she resents this constant imposition, and does not think it's fair that she's expected to be so involved in the children's lives.

Albelli indicates a similarly close proximity to her wards: the image of the young boy "curled" around her leg is a symbol of the closeness between them. However, she uses rhetorical questions to suggest that this closeness is desirable, which challenges negative attitudes such as Brontë's. She questions "How can Mary Poppins be indifferent?", to suggest that nannies should aim to be close to children in their care, even whilst maintaining some degree of professional detachment.

This answer gets ☐ marks out of 16 because ....
....
....
....
....

Paper 2, Question 5 — Mark Scheme

It's time for a 40-marker... crikey. These sample answers are for question 5 — the non-fiction writing task.

Have another look at question 5

| 0 | 5 | "In order to prepare young adults for the challenges of raising a family, it should be made compulsory for them to spend time volunteering with young children."

Write a speech, to be given to your local council, in which you argue your point of view on this statement.

(24 marks for content and organisation
16 marks for technical accuracy)

[40 marks]

Question 5 tests your writing abilities

1) Question 5 tests <u>two</u> separate criteria:

   • There are 24 marks for writing <u>interesting content</u> that is <u>well-organised</u>.

   • There are another 16 marks for <u>technical accuracy</u>, including <u>spelling</u>, <u>punctuation</u> and <u>grammar</u>.

2) A really good answer to this question will be <u>clear</u>, <u>imaginative</u> and <u>interesting</u> — for example, it could use <u>rhetorical devices</u> and varied <u>sentence forms</u> to argue its viewpoint.

3) The writing style of the answer needs to be matched to the <u>form</u>, <u>purpose</u> and <u>audience</u> specified in the question — it should be clear that it's a <u>speech</u>, it needs to successfully <u>argue</u> a point of view, and it needs to be appropriate for an audience of <u>local council members</u>.

Here's the mark scheme for question 5

This table will help you to mark the answers on the next page.

	Content and organisation		Technical accuracy
19-24 marks Level 4	Imaginative use of structure and language techniques, thoroughly matched to form, purpose and audience.	13-16 marks Level 4	Ambitious use of vocabulary; confidently uses a wide range of grammar and punctuation.
13-18 marks Level 3	Effective writing, using a clear structure and language techniques. Matched to form, purpose and audience.	9-12 marks Level 3	Largely suitable, varied vocabulary; a range of mostly correct grammar and punctuation.
7-12 marks Level 2	Mostly matched to form, purpose and audience. Some language techniques and structural features.	5-8 marks Level 2	Attempts a variety of vocabulary, punctuation and grammar, sometimes successfully.
1-6 marks Level 1	Some sense of purpose, a few relevant ideas linked together, a mostly disorganised structure.	1-4 marks Level 1	Simple vocabulary, grammar and punctuation are used with inaccuracies throughout.

Paper 2, Question 5 — Sample Answers

Here are two <u>extracts</u> from sample answers to question 5.

1) Make sure you've <u>read</u> the <u>advice</u> and <u>mark scheme</u> on page 88.
2) Mark each of the criteria <u>separately</u>, then <u>add</u> up the marks to get a total out of 40.
3) <u>Explain</u> how you've decided on the marks in the lines below the answers.

These answers are extracts again, but you should still give them a mark out of 40.

Answer 1

| 0 | 5 |

    In a nutshell, the idea of a Young People's Volunteer Programme is a deeply flawed concept. Whilst volunteering with children is undoubtedly an effective way for young people to experience the trials of parenthood, the Programme has a number of practical and logistical difficulties, which shed serious doubt on its advisability.

    Young people simply do not have time to volunteer. They are already ground to the bone, juggling home life and academics in the hope of getting that important first job. Moreover, the assumption that all young people will one day have children is outdated; up to 10% of young people say that they do not wish to become a parent. Thirdly, and perhaps most importantly, humans have raised children since time began. Why waste time when we are evolutionarily primed to be good parents?

Content and organisation = ☐ / 24 ....

Technical accuracy = ☐ / 16 ....

Total = ☐ / 40 ....

Answer 2

| 0 | 5 |

    Hello, I think it's a good idea to make young people volunteer with children. Not just because they need to be prepared if they become parents one day — it's just generally really good for you to hang around with children sometimes.

    The positive side of the argument is that when you work with children, you start to develop important skills like selflessness, good communication and imaginative thinking. These are all really important, to being a parent, but also in the workplace and in other areas of life. Some people would probably disagree with me. It's tough to find the time to volunteer, and I suppose the programme will probably turn out to be quite expensive. But its worth it in my opinion — if I'm right, then the future will be full of happy children, raised by experienced parents.

Content and organisation = ☐ / 24 ....

Technical accuracy = ☐ / 16 ....

Total = ☐ / 40 ....

Paper 1 — Questions

This section has two <u>practice exam papers</u> in it — they're similar in style to the two exams you'll take for your AQA GCSE in English Language.

To start with, have a look at this practice exam for <u>paper 1</u> (called 'Explorations in Creative Reading and Writing'). Try to practise answering these questions as if you were in a <u>real</u> exam — give yourself <u>1 hour 45 minutes</u> to read through the source and answer all five questions.

Section A — Reading

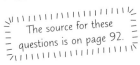
The source for these questions is on page 92.

> *You should spend about 15 minutes reading the source and all the questions.*
>
> *Then you should spend about 45 minutes answering **all** the questions in this section.*

0 1   Read again the first part of the source, **lines 1 to 11**.

List **four** things from this part of the text that show what Crescent Bay looks like beneath the mist.

[4 marks]

0 2   Look in detail at **lines 16 to 22** of the source.

How does the writer use language here to describe the shepherd and his animals?

You could include the writer's choice of:

- words and phrases
- language features and techniques
- sentence forms.

[8 marks]

0 3   You now need to think about the **whole** of the **source**.

This text is from the opening of a short story.

How has the writer structured the text to interest you as a reader?

You could write about:

- what the writer focuses your attention on at the beginning
- how and why the writer changes this focus as the extract develops
- any other structural features that interest you.

[8 marks]

Paper 1 — Questions

0 4 | Focus this part of your answer on the second half of the source, from **line 23 to the end**.

A student, having read this section of the text said "The writer is successful in creating a detailed and interesting scene for the reader. It is like watching a film of what is happening."

To what extent do you agree?

In your response, you could:

- write about your own impressions of the scene
- evaluate how the writer has created these impressions
- support your opinions with references to the text.

[20 marks]

Section B — Writing

You should spend about 45 minutes answering the question in this section.
You are advised to plan your answer.

0 5 | A publisher is running a creative writing competition for school children, which you have decided to enter.

Your entry will be judged by a panel of published authors.

Either:

Write a description suggested by this picture:

© iStockphoto.com/Empato

Or:

Write the opening part of a story that takes place in a misty setting.

(24 marks for content and organisation
16 marks for technical accuracy)

[40 marks]

Paper 1 — Exam Source

This extract is the opening of a short story set in New Zealand, written in 1922 by Katherine Mansfield.

At the Bay

Very early morning. The sun was not yet risen, and the whole of Crescent Bay was hidden under a white sea-mist. The big bush-covered hills at the back were smothered. You could not see where they ended and the paddocks and bungalows began. The sandy road was gone and the paddocks and bungalows the other side of it; there were no white dunes covered with reddish grass beyond them;
5 there was nothing to mark which was beach and where was the sea. A heavy dew had fallen. The grass was blue. Big drops hung on the bushes and just did not fall; the silvery, fluffy toi-toi* was limp on its long stalks, and all the marigolds and the pinks in the bungalow gardens were bowed to the earth with wetness. Drenched were the cold fuchsias, round pearls of dew lay on the flat nasturtium leaves. It looked as though the sea had beaten up softly in the darkness, as though one immense wave had come
10 rippling, rippling — how far? Perhaps if you had waked up in the middle of the night you might have seen a big fish flicking in at the window and gone again...

Ah-Aah! sounded the sleepy sea. And from the bush there came the sound of little streams flowing, quickly, lightly, slipping between the smooth stones, gushing into ferny basins and out again; and there was the splashing of big drops on large leaves, and something else — what was it? — a faint stirring and
15 shaking, the snapping of a twig and then such silence that it seemed some one was listening.

Round the corner of Crescent Bay, between the piled-up masses of broken rock, a flock of sheep came pattering. They were huddled together, a small, tossing, woolly mass, and their thin, stick-like legs trotted along quickly as if the cold and the quiet had frightened them. Behind them an old sheep-dog, his soaking paws covered with sand, ran along with his nose to the ground, but carelessly,
20 as if thinking of something else. And then in the rocky gateway the shepherd himself appeared. He was a lean, upright old man, in a frieze** coat that was covered with a web of tiny drops, velvet trousers tied under the knee, and a wide-awake*** with a folded blue handkerchief round the brim.

One hand was crammed into his belt, the other grasped a beautifully smooth yellow stick. And as he walked, taking his time, he kept up a very soft light whistling, an airy, far-away fluting that sounded
25 mournful and tender. The old dog cut an ancient caper or two and then drew up sharp, ashamed of his levity, and walked a few dignified paces by his master's side. The sheep ran forward in little pattering rushes; they began to bleat, and ghostly flocks and herds answered them from under the sea. "Baa! Baaa!" For a time they seemed to be always on the same piece of ground. There ahead was stretched the sandy road with shallow puddles; the same soaking bushes showed on either side and the same
30 shadowy palings****. Then something immense came into view; an enormous shock-haired giant with his arms stretched out. It was the big gum-tree outside Mrs. Stubbs' shop, and as they passed by there was a strong whiff of eucalyptus. And now big spots of light gleamed in the mist. The shepherd stopped whistling; he rubbed his red nose and wet beard on his wet sleeve and, screwing up his eyes, glanced in the direction of the sea. The sun was rising. It was marvellous how quickly the mist
35 thinned, sped away, dissolved from the shallow plain, rolled up from the bush and was gone as if in a hurry to escape; big twists and curls jostled and shouldered each other as the silvery beams broadened. The far-away sky — a bright, pure blue — was reflected in the puddles, and the drops, swimming along the telegraph poles, flashed into points of light. Now the leaping, glittering sea was so bright it made one's eyes ache to look at it. The shepherd drew a pipe, the bowl as small as an acorn, out of his
40 breast pocket, fumbled for a chunk of speckled tobacco, pared off a few shavings and stuffed the bowl. He was a grave, fine-looking old man. As he lit up and the blue smoke wreathed his head, the dog, watching, looked proud of him.

Glossary
*toi-toi — a type of tall grass
**frieze — coarse woollen cloth
***wide-awake — a type of wide-brimmed hat
****palings — pointed fence-posts

Paper 2 — Questions

This practice exam is similar in style to paper 2 ('Writers' Viewpoints and Perspectives') of your AQA GCSE in English Language. To make the most of these questions, read the sources and do the questions as if you were in the exam, giving yourself 1 hour 45 minutes to complete the lot.

Section A — Reading

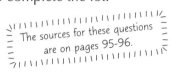
The sources for these questions are on pages 95-96.

You should spend about 15 minutes reading the sources and all the questions.

*Then you should spend about 45 minutes answering **all** the questions in this section.*

0 1 Read again **source A**, from lines 1 to 19.

Choose **four** statements below which are TRUE.

- Shade the boxes of the ones that you think are true
- Choose a maximum of four statements.

A   Jo is more hurt by Genevieve's lies than by her cancelling their plans.   ☐

B   Genevieve tells Jo that she is going to a formal dinner party.   ☐

C   Jo relies on her long-term friendships.   ☐

D   Jo calls Jenni to tell her about her friendship troubles.   ☐

E   Jo is upset to see Genevieve when she arrives at the dinner party.   ☐

F   Jo thinks honesty is a minor part of a friendship.   ☐

G   Jo doesn't like to talk about her feelings with her friends.   ☐

H   Losing Genevieve as a friend is a significant moment in Jo's life.   ☐

[4 marks]

0 2 You need to refer to **source A** and **source B** for this question.

Use details from **both** sources. Write a summary of the differences between Genevieve and the Boisterous Friend.

[8 marks]

0 3 You now need to refer **only** to **source B**, lines 1 to 8.

How does the beggar use language to try to influence his listeners?

[12 marks]

Paper 2 — Questions

0 4   For this question you need to refer to **source A** and **source B**.

Compare how Jenni Russell and Wilkie Collins convey their different attitudes to friendship.

In your answer, you could:

- compare their different attitudes
- compare the methods they use to convey their attitudes
- support your ideas with references to both texts.

[16 marks]

Section B — Writing

You should spend about 45 minutes answering the question in this section.
You are advised to plan your answer.

0 5   "It is worrying that many people today place so much importance on their 'friends' from social media platforms. Real friendships can only be made face-to-face."

Write an article for a broadsheet newspaper in which you explain your point of view on this statement.

(24 marks for content and organisation
16 marks for technical accuracy)

[40 marks]

Ralph and Bernard felt that real friendships were best made back-to-back.

Paper 2 — Exam Source A

The following text is an extract from an article in a broadsheet newspaper by a journalist called Jenni Russell. It was published in 2005.

What are friends for?

Earlier this year, I rang my friend Jo and found her in a state of stunned misery.

Jo is a witty, sexy, single, childless woman in her 40s. She's a talented artist, but earns very little. Without a career, money, husband or family to bolster her confidence, a small group of friends have been a key part of her identity. Genevieve, an ambitious, glamorous woman whom she met at
5   university, has been her constant confidante* for almost a quarter of a century. But in the past three or four years, Genevieve has become increasingly unreliable: making dates she later cancels; slow to return calls or emails.

Last winter, Jo arranged for them to go to a film together, only for Genevieve to ring at 6pm to say she was awfully sorry, but she had to spend the evening with some dreary Burmese** refugees, friends
10   of her father's. Fortunately for Jo, 20 minutes later she was rung and asked to make up the numbers for a formal dinner party. When she walked into the room, she felt as if she had been punched in the stomach. Genevieve was sitting on the sofa, flirting with the men on either side of her. There were no refugees.

"The next day I sent her an email saying: 'Why did you lie to me? Why not just say: I want to go to
15   a dinner party? I can take that. I can't take being lied to. This is a friendship. We're supposed to trust one another.' She emailed back immediately saying she didn't have to explain herself to me. And then a month later she said our friendship had run its course, and she wouldn't be seeing me any more. It's one of the worst things that's ever happened to me. And I haven't just lost her; I've lost all our history, all that shared experience."

20   Often, we don't know where we fit into friends' lives. Are we in the first dozen, or the remotest 90 in their circle? If they ask us to dinner once a year, is that an honour because they only entertain twice, or a sign of our unimportance, because they hold dinners every week?

This degree of uncertainty exists partly because many of us now lead lives in which we are the only connecting thread. It is perfectly possible for much of our lives to be opaque to anyone who knows us.
25   They may only ever encounter one particular facet of our existence, because we can, if we choose, keep parents, past acquaintances, old partners, colleagues, friends, and neighbours in totally separate boxes. Many people value the anonymity and freedom that gives them. The flip side is that just as we are not known, so we cannot really know others.

Talking to a wide range of people, it was clear that few of them are really happy with the friendships
30   they have. People with consuming jobs are sad that they haven't had the time to build stronger bonds, and wonder whether it's too late to develop them; mothers with time to spare want to find new friends but don't know how. Many people would like to have more friends, or deeper, warmer, more reliable relationships than the ones they have now, but don't know how to go about it.

There are powerful reasons why we should create these bonds, even if we only start when we are
35   older. The phenomenon of later births means families take up a smaller percentage of our lives. We wait years to have children, and we could be 70 before we become grandparents for the first time. We have more time available, and fewer familial responsibilities, than the generations before us. We all want to feel needed and valued by others. It is possible for friends to fill that need, but only if we work at it.

40   It isn't easy, because friendship is a subtle dance, and no one wants to be explicitly pursued when it's unwelcome, or explicitly dropped when they are not wanted. Nor does it come with any guarantees. People are unpredictable. But we need to play the game of friendship. Evidence shows that people with close friends live longer and are happier than those without. And friendship defines what it means to be human.

Glossary
*confidante — a close friend; someone you talk to about private matters
**Burmese — people from a country in southeast Asia that's currently known as Burma or Myanmar

Paper 2 — Exam Source B

This is an extract from a piece by Wilkie Collins, which appeared in a periodical called 'Household Words' in 1858. A periodical was a collection of fiction and non-fiction that related to the topics of the day, published once a week or once a month (similar to a modern magazine). Collins has just described a beggar addressing a crowd in the street — this extract starts with his report of the beggar's speech.

Save me from my friends

"Good Christian people, will you be so obliging as to leave off your various occupations for a few minutes only, and listen to the harrowing statement of a father of a family, who is reduced to acknowledge his misfortunes in the public streets? Work, honest work, is all I ask for; and I cannot get it. Good Christian people, I think it is because I have no friends. Alas! I assure you I am right in saying, because

5   we have no friends. Why am I and my wife and my seven babes starving in a land of plenty? Why am I injured by being deprived of work when I ask for it? Why have I no share in the wholesome necessaries of life, which I see, with my hungry eyes, in butchers' and bakers' shops on each side of me? Must I perish in a land of plenty because I have no work and because I have no friends?"

"No friends!" I repeated to myself, as I walked away. But can the marvellous assertion be true? Can

10   this enviable man really go home and touch up his speech for to-morrow, with the certainty of not being interrupted? I am going home to finish an article, without knowing whether I shall have a clear five minutes to myself, all the time I am at work. Can he take his money back to his drawer, in broad daylight, and meet nobody by the way who will say to him, 'Remember our old friendship, and lend me a trifle'? I have money waiting for me at my publisher's, and I dare not go to fetch it, except under cover of the night.

15   No wonder that he looks prosperous and healthy, though he lives in a dingy slum, and that I look peevish and pale, though I reside on gravel, in an airy neighbourhood.

It is a dreadful thing to say (even anonymously); but it is the sad truth that I could positively dispense with a great many of my dearest friends.

There is my Boisterous Friend, for instance. I always know when he calls, though my study is at the

20   top of the house. I hear him in the passage, the moment the door is opened. I have told my servant to say that I am engaged, which means simply, that I am hard at work. "Dear old boy!" I hear my Boisterous Friend exclaim, with a genial roar, "writing away, the jolly, hard-working, clever old chap, just as usual — eh, Susan? Lord bless you! he knows me — he knows I don't want to interrupt him." My door is burst open, as if with a battering-ram (no boisterous man ever knocks), and my friend rushes in like a mad bull.

25   "Ha, ha, ha! I've caught you," says the associate of my childhood. "Don't stop for me, dear old boy; I'm not going to interrupt you (Lord bless my soul, what a lot of writing!) — and you're all right, eh? No! I won't sit down; I won't stop another instant. So glad to have seen you dear fellow — good bye." By this time, his affectionate voice has made the room ring again; he has squeezed my hand, in his brotherly way, till my fingers are too sore to hold the pen; and he has put to flight, for the rest of the day, every idea that I

30   had when I sat down to work. Could I really dispense with him? I don't deny that he has known me from the time when I was in short frocks*, and that he loves me like a brother. Nevertheless, I could dispense — yes, I could dispense — oh, yes, I could dispense — with my Boisterous Friend.

I have not by any means done yet with the number of my dear friends whom I could dispense with. To say nothing of my friend who borrows money of me (an obvious nuisance), there is my self-satisfied

35   friend, who can talk of nothing but himself, and his successes in life; there is my inattentive friend, who is perpetually asking me irrelevant questions, and who has no power of listening to my answers; there is my hospitable friend, who is continually telling me that he wants so much to ask me to dinner, and who never does really ask me by any chance.

A double knock at the street door stops my pen suddenly. A well-known voice in the passage smites

40   my ear, inquiring for me, on very particular business, and asking the servant to take in the name. No necessity, Susan, to mention the name; I have recognised the voice. This is my friend who does not at all like the state of my health. Well, well, I have made my confession, and eased my mind. Show him in, Susan — show him in.

Glossary
*short frocks — the short dresses that very young children (both male and female) would be dressed in

Answers

Section One — Exam Basics

Page 1: Planning Answers

1. a) lines 12-21
   b) Uncle William
   c) language
2. Here are some things you could mention:
   * The plan is well-structured to explain a point of view.
   * Includes arguments and counter arguments.
   * All points are relevant to the question.
   * Gives examples to help illustrate points.
   * Conclusion gives an opinion on the statement.
   * Conclusion clearly summarises the argument.
   * Conclusion answers the question.
3. E.g. Para 1: Pets are a huge responsibility — risk that pupils might neglect them.
   Para 2: Unfair on parents, who will be forced to help students out.
   Para 3: Would also strain school budgets (give statistics).
   Conclusion: Should look for other ways to teach students responsibility.

Pages 2-3: P.E.E.D.

1. a) and c) should be ticked.
2. a) Example: e.g. "you can become a real-life tomb explorer"
   Explanation: e.g. makes the reader feel like they can get involved with the experience.
   b) Example: "explore, quest and hunt"
   Explanation: e.g. makes the experience seem continuously action-filled.
3. a) Any sensible answer, e.g. "determined".
   b) Any example that is relevant to the answer in a), e.g. "she was going to do it her way and it'd be all the better for it"
   c) Answers need to explain the example in b), e.g. "This quote suggests that Alice is a strong-willed character who isn't afraid to take an independent approach."
   d) Answers should develop the answer in c), e.g. "Alice's determination to plan her own trip may also suggest that she'll have some interesting experiences, which draws the reader into the story."

Pages 4-5: Writing Well

1. a) Overall, the writer in Source A demonstrates a more positive attitude towards breeding cats.
   b) The writer in Source B doesn't include other people's point of view, so they're very biased.
   c) The writer in Source B tries to convince the reader using an anecdote about cat breeding.
2. a) E.g. The metaphor "a furious battleground" suggests that the house is very chaotic.
   b) E.g. The conversation between Sam and Nina tells you how the characters are feeling.
3. reinforce; Furthermore; emphasises; signifying
4. Another point of view is, Secondly, In addition to this, Conversely
5. Paragraph breaks should be inserted as below. Phrases in bold can be substituted for any other sensible linking phrase.
   The extract from the biography argues that Orson Welles' career was a "magnificent failure". It points to the fact that his greatest achievement, 'Citizen Kane', was made before the age of thirty.
   In contrast, the magazine article argues that Orson Welles was a wonderful director and actor throughout his career. It suggests that people like the "myth" of Orson Welles' fall from grace and ignore his later achievements.

Finally, the third text, the interview with Orson Welles, shows that he himself had conflicting feelings towards his career and achievements. The interviewer describes him as "fiercely proud" of his films, but also "insecure beneath the bravado".

Pages 6-7: Reading with Insight

1. a) The character is looking forward to something.
   b) The character is feeling exhausted.
   c) The character is feeling uncomfortable.
2. Words and phrases which imply the writer dislikes Hitchcock's later films could include:
   * leaden in pace and tone
   * increasingly dull
   * self-conscious style of film
   Words and phrases which imply the writer likes Hitchcock's early films could include:
   * still delight
   * wonderful humour
   * lightness of touch
   * masterpieces
   Words and phrases which imply the writer dislikes Hitchcock as a person could include:
   * gorged himself
   * substantial ego
3. Example: e.g. "cheated"
   Explanation: e.g. "The writer uses this word to emphasise how they feel they've been misled by the restaurant owner, which is intended to make the restaurant owner feel guilty."
4. Answers must be backed up with relevant evidence, e.g.
   Ed is feeling nervous in this passage, which is suggested by his body language: the writer says he "shifted his weight from one foot to the other" and "He took a deep breath". This sense of nervousness is reinforced using the passage's dialogue: the woman says that Ed looks "a bit peaky".

Pages 8-9: Spelling, Punctuation and Grammar

1. a) I jumped out of the taxi, narrowly missing a very large puddle by the kerb.
   b) Keeley said she wanted a tablet, a pair of shoes and some more make-up.
   c) As the boat glided past, its bright paint glinting in the sun, I was able to see the captain saluting me, his gold braid fluttering in the breeze.
2. Answers that should be ticked:
   unnatural, disappear, immediately, occasional
   Answers that should be corrected:
   arguement — argument
   neccessarily — necessarily
   favorite — favourite
   embarassed — embarrassed
   concsious — conscious
   decieved — deceived
   figarative — figurative
   consience — conscience
3. a) I didn't want to go; the leaden sky threatened rain.
   b) Have you ever wondered what it would be like to travel in time? It'd be fantastic!
   c) You can come to my party as long as you bring an expensive present, lovingly wrapped; stay until the end, which will be 2 am; clear up any spillages; and serve the drinks.
4. a) E.g. There was no reason to have a fire drill during the exam.
   b) E.g. Hannah should have eaten the sandwich before its expiry date.

Answers

5.   As he stepped out of the exam hall on that <u>T</u>uesday morning, Rashid breathed an enormous sigh of relief. He wouldn't need to do <u>any</u> more practice papers, and his days of revision and stress were finished. He could <u>have</u> shouted with joy. It was over, and <u>hopefully</u> it had been worth it. He felt the scientific equations <u>evaporate</u> from his mind like morning dew. As Rashid leant gently against the wall to steady himself, he was overcome by the <u>knowledge</u> that his life was now his. He <u>wasn't</u> sure exactly what it would bring, but that was part of the excitement<u>.</u>

Section Two — Reading — Understanding Texts

Pages 10-11: Finding Information and Ideas

1. b) Dani is nervous about going on the roller coaster.
2.   Last weekend we found ourselves with nothing to do on a warm, sunny day, so we decided on a trip to the zoo. The entrance to the zoo was via a <u>rusty</u> iron gate that looked <u>in serious need of repair</u>. We went into the ticket office, only to discover that <u>the floor was filthy</u>; as we looked closer, we realised <u>there was revolting leftover food scattered everywhere</u>. Inside, the animals looked <u>malnourished and miserable</u> in their enclosures, which all seemed <u>dull and empty</u>, with <u>precious little space</u> for them to run around. All in all, <u>a pretty depressing place</u>.
3. Any three correct facts about the garden, either paraphrased or directly quoted, and from the correct part of the text. For example:
   - There is a bench in the garden.
   - The bench takes up most of the space in the garden.
   - The garden is tiny.
   - There is a fence in the garden.
   - The fence has gaps in it.
   - There is grass in the garden.
   - The grass is damp.
   - There is an apple tree in the garden.
   - The apple tree is in the corner of the garden.
4. Any four correct facts about George, either paraphrased or directly quoted from the text. For example:
   - George has a nasal voice.
   - George has a loud voice.
   - George is wearing a "garish purple suit".
   - George has an "elaborate hairstyle".
   - George brings a bottle of wine to the party.
   - George has "greasy" hands.
   - George is wearing several rings.
   - George likes whisky.
5. The following four statements should be ticked:
   - On the second day, the writer got up early.
   - The writer enjoyed the pony trek.
   - You can abseil at Lowbridge Park.
   - The writer liked the archery instructor.

Pages 12-13: Summarising Information and Ideas

1. a) Rita
   E.g. "It's bad enough that we have to go at all", "If it were up to me, we'd never have agreed to go."
   b) Rita
   E.g. "We're going to be late, Samuel", "Rita glared pointedly at her watch", "we're going to show up late, too".
   c) Samuel
   E.g. "We'll be fine!", "triumphantly", "admiring his reflection", "It'll be fun!"
2. Meat Eaters: Eating meat is natural for human beings and is important for human health.

Vegetarians: Eating meat is unnatural for human beings and can cause health problems.

3. Answers should analyse both texts, using relevant quotes from both texts to summarise several differences between the writers. Here are some things you could mention:
   - The writer in Source A is more shocked ("simply astonished") by child poverty than in Source B ("it's not that surprising given the state of the area in general").
   - The writer in Source A believes that it's partly their responsibility to help the orphans ("it is our duty as their fellow men"), whereas the writer in Source B believes the opposite ("it shouldn't be my job to help them").
   - The writer in Source A appears to be fairly wealthy ("investing our funds"), but the writer in Source B is not ("even if I had money to give").
4. Answers should analyse both texts, using relevant quotes from both texts to summarise several differences between the writers. Here are some things you could mention:
   - The writer in Source B believes that men and women have equal importance in a marriage ("a partnership of equals"), whereas the writer in Source A prioritises the man ("amenable to the needs of the husband").
   - The writer in Source A says that women belong at home ("The home is her sphere"), but the writer in Source B does not ("most women today would spurn the idea that they should... take sole care of a home").
   - The writer in Source A believes that a perfect home is one where the husband does no housework ("need not lift a finger"), but the writer in Source B thinks that a perfect home involves sharing it equally ("it is essential for domestic responsibilities to be shared evenly").

Pages 14-15: Audience and Purpose

1. a) adults   b) novices
2. a) To advise   b) To entertain   c) To persuade
3. E.g.
   Word or phrase: "earn a few quid"
   Explanation: Uses slang in order to relate to the reader.
   Word or phrase: "find us on social media."
   Explanation: Refers to something used regularly by young people to suggest that the company is modern and fun.
4. All your points should use relevant examples and terminology, and comment on the effects of the language used. Here are some things you could mention:
   - Use of puns / wordplay to make the attraction seem fun, e.g. "you'll have a whale of a time", "shaken by a shark", which attracts young people's attention in particular.
   - Uses the phrase "special underwater world" to appeal to a younger audience's sense of adventure.
   - Mentions school and school holidays ("we're open every day in the school holidays") to show that they cater to young people's needs.
   - Uses testimonials from other young people to suggest that the aquarium is an enjoyable experience for a young person.
5. All your points should use relevant examples and terminology, and comment on the effects of the language used. Here are some things you could mention:
   - Use of rhetorical questions ("Is it really that time of year again?") to engage the reader.
   - Use of hyperbole ("whipped up into a frenzy", "sudden and deathly terror") to add humour and keep the reader interested in the article.
   - Use of a simile ("like headless chickens") to add humour and make panic shopping seem ridiculous.
   - First-person viewpoint used to create a personal tone so the reader relates to the writer and their viewpoint.

Answers

- Use of direct address ("Britain, we need to take a stand") to draw the reader in and make authoritative remarks that persuade them to agree with the writer.

Pages 16-17: Informative and Entertaining Texts

1. a) I b) E c) I
2. E.g. The first sentence ("The woman was incredibly old.") is short and direct, creating a sense of drama that engages the reader. The phrase "clink and clank" is onomatopoeic, which appeals to the reader's senses to help them imagine the scene.
3. a) Two of the following:
   - There are eight thermal pools.
   - Each pool is a different temperature.
   - The temperature of the hottest pool is 40 degrees.
   b) E.g. The writer describes the hottest pool as "immersive", helping the reader to imagine it as an intense experience.
4. Your answer should offer an opinion on the statement. It should comment on the techniques the writer uses to make the text entertaining and to present the character, using relevant examples and terminology to support each point.
   Here are some things you could mention:
   - Humorous images such as having to be "surgically removed from her game console" are entertaining for the reader, and show Jasmine's addictive personality.
   - The use of hyperbole to establish that Jasmine has a humorously over-dramatic personality — "more daunting than an icy trek over an arctic precipice".
   - Narrative viewpoint allows the reader an insight into Jasmine's thoughts, e.g. "Those girls terrified her", which suggests that she may be shy — this hint at another side to her personality adds interest for the reader.
   - Ironic metaphors to highlight Jasmine's stubborn personality in a humorous way — "all the staunch tenacity of an Olympic athlete".
5. All your points should use relevant examples and terminology, and comment on the effects of the language used. Here are some things you could mention:
   - The inclusion of informative dates and facts — "The Battle of Hastings was fought on October 14th 1066".
   - Statements such as "it was the Normans' most important victory over the Anglo-Saxons", which are used to convey information in a clear, direct way.
   - The use of a simile ("trampled like insects") to make the text more entertaining to read.
   - The use of descriptive verbs such as "stormed" and "ambushed" to create a sense of action and excitement, increasing the entertainment value for the reader.

Pages 18-19: Texts that Argue, Persuade or Advise

1. a) To argue b) To advise c) To persuade
2.

Technique	Example from text
rhetorical question	Should such beauty go unsupported?
opinion stated as fact	Flamingos are the most fascinating birds in the world. OR Their beguiling beauty is unrivalled in the animal kingdom.
expert opinion	Flamingos really are wonderful animals. OR A dedicated breeding programme would be invaluable to their endurance as a species.
direct address to the reader	you can help fund the establishment of breeding programmes

3. Example: e.g. "you could consider"
   Explanation: e.g. It reassures the reader that the text is giving helpful suggestions, not authoritative commands.

4. All your points should use relevant examples and terminology, and comment on the effects of the language used. Here are some things you could mention:
   - Opening rhetorical question ("But Who Do I Vote For?") suggests that the writer is on the reader's side.
   - Casual style to make the reader comfortable, e.g. "Unless you've been living under a rock for the past month".
   - Use of the imperative form ("don't panic", "have a look") to give clear guidance to the reader.
   - Minimal technical language to avoid intimidating or confusing the reader.
   - Introductory/concluding paragraphs create a clear structure and summarise the information to make it easier for the reader to understand.
5. All your points should use relevant examples and terminology, and comment on the effects of the language used. Here are some things you could mention:
   - Strong descriptive vocabulary such as "horrified", "dangerous" and "fatal" to convey the idea that Swampy Water is a bad product.
   - Suggestion that the writer is an expert so that the reader is more likely to agree with them: "I know from my time in the Territorial Army".
   - Lists all of the arguments in one paragraph, linked by words like "Firstly", "Secondly" and "Finally" to give the impression that there are lots of good arguments in the writer's favour.
   - Presents the opinion of the writer as fact ("clearly idiotic", "any sane parent would endorse") to make the reader think that the writer's opinion is valid.

Pages 20-21: Writer's Viewpoint and Attitude

1. a) negative b) positive c) balanced
2. a) iii) b) iv) c) ii) d) i)
3. Answers need to use examples from both texts to summarise a similarity and a difference between their views, e.g.
   The writers agree that mobile phones should be banned from lessons. Source A says that they are a "nightmare" for teachers, and the writer in Source B is "not about to suggest" they should be allowed in lessons either.
   The writers disagree that mobile phones should be banned from school entirely. The first writer says it's the "best way" to prevent the disruptions, but the second writer believes there's no "harm" in them being used at lunchtimes.
4. Answers should clearly compare the different ideas and techniques in each text, using quotations to support points. Here are some things you could mention:
   - In Source A, the writer illustrates their dislike of a new art style using hyperbole ("nothing short of an abomination"). In Source B, the writer expresses their admiration for a new art style, also using hyperbole ("They're revolutionaries").
   - Both sources use formal language, e.g. "I read with concern" in Source A, "progression in the medium" in Source B. This makes their opinion seem more important / authoritative.
   - Source B makes the restrictions of traditional art seem negative using a metaphor, "the iron shackles of 'traditional art'", whereas Source A thinks that the rules of traditional art are good: new artists should have "learnt from" older examples.

Answers

5. Answers should clearly compare the different ideas and techniques in each text, using quotations to support points. Here are some things you could mention:
    *   The sources use figurative language to convey their different emotions about rail transport. Source A uses a simile to make the steam train seem new and exciting: "shiny as a new penny", whilst Source B uses a metaphor to compare the passing trains to a "non-stop army", which makes them seem relentless and invasive.
    *   Source B is trying to persuade the audience, so it uses rhetorical devices such as repetition ("like me") and direct address ("Residents of Station Crescent!") in an attempt to engage them. Source A is a diary, so it doesn't contain any overtly persuasive language. It's more descriptive, e.g. "curled into the summer sky".
    *   Both sources make use of exclamation marks. In Source A they're used to convey the writer's excitement at seeing a steam train, whilst in Source B they're used to prompt an emotion in the audience and persuade them to agree with the speaker.

Pages 22-23: Literary Fiction and Literary Non-Fiction

1. a) 3   b) 1   c) 2
2. a)   As I stared at the letter, no longer absorbing the words on the page, I realised my hands were starting to shake. How dare they! After all I'd done for that family... their betrayal cut me like a knife. Without even realising it, I'd begun to tear the paper into pieces; ripping, shredding, mutilating the letter until I was left with a pile of limp paper-snowflakes. Then, just for good measure, I aimed a sharp kick at the pile, scattering it across the carpet.
    b) Answers should explain how one of the underlined phrases above creates an impression of the narrator's anger. E.g. The writer uses an exclamation, "How dare they!", to emphasise the writer's sense of injustice.
3. fact; biographies; purpose; argument; entertain; dialogue
4. Your answer should comment on the techniques used to present the characters, using relevant examples and terminology. Here are some things you could mention:
    *   The use of dialogue to give an insight into each character's mindset, such as Annie: "Don't be ridiculous." and Lucas: "They'll kill me." This indicates that Annie is calmer and less prone to being overdramatic in comparison to Lucas.
    *   The cumulative use of short sentences in Lucas's speech to emphasise his stress, e.g. "I've looked everywhere. It's lost. They'll kill me."
    *   The contrast between the two characters, which makes each character's personalities stand out more. E.g. the adjectives used to describe Lucas's actions ("frantic", "manic") contrast with the adverbs used to describe Annie's actions, which are carried out "cautiously" or "calmly".
5. Answers should clearly compare the different ideas and techniques in each text, using quotations to support points. Here are some things you could mention:
    *   The two sources use very different tones to convey their attitudes. Source A has an emphatic tone — it uses the word "must" twice, which emphasises the inflexibility of his beliefs. Source B is less direct: it conveys its viewpoint using anecdotal evidence.
    *   Source A uses an analogy to convey the idea that teaching should be very strict and disciplined — he compares the "schoolmaster" to a "military officer" and pupils to "troops", which suggests that he believes schools should be run as strictly as armies.

*   Source B also believes discipline is important — from the "indistinct" memories of the writer's past, it is the memory of his strict teacher that stands out the most: it is still "clear as day" to him. This simile indicates that Mr Wan was the most important thing about the writer's time at school.
*   Source A suggests that conveying an "academic education" to pupils is the ultimate goal for a teacher, but in Source B the narrator implies that "the priceless lesson of human decency" is the most important thing he learned during his school days.

Pages 24-25: 19th-Century Texts

1. a) Catherine is Sir Edward's niece.
    b) The Spears family, because Albert Withers was ill.
    c) "an agreeable gathering" or "much happiness felt by all involved"
2. a) E.g. The writer thinks that social class is very important, and that people from different social classes shouldn't mix.
    b) E.g. The writer thinks that sending children away to boarding school is necessary, but personally, she finds it emotionally difficult.
3. All your points should use relevant examples and terminology, and comment on the effects of the language used. Here are some things you could mention:
    *   Regular reminders of the relationship between the writer and her daughter: "doting and loving mother", "your poor mother". These are intended to make the writer's daughter feel guilty.
    *   The use of direct address to persuade the writer's daughter, e.g. "I implore you", whilst also appearing reasonable, e.g. "I do not write to you to chastise".
    *   Rhetorical questions, which make the writer's daughter think carefully about her actions — "How do you imagine I would survive the shock?"
4. All your points should use relevant examples and terminology, and comment on the effects of the language used. Here are some things you could mention:
    *   Appealing to the audience by using flattering language, such as "wise and influential persons". This might make the audience like the speaker, which would mean they are more likely to be persuaded by him.
    *   Emotive language, such as "poor Tommy" and "condemn", to appeal to the audience's sense of compassion and persuade them that the speaker's cause is "just".
    *   Repetition of the word "fight", which is a call to action. The repetition gives it greater emphasis, so it might rouse some listeners to join the speaker's cause.

Section Three — Reading — Language and Structure

Pages 26-27: Tone, Style and Register

1. a) angry   b) detached   c) upbeat   d) sentimental
2. a) "Customers are advised that we do not accept credit cards."
    b) "It is essential to ensure you have the correct tools before proceeding."
    c) "If you have financial complications, contact our trained advisors."
3. Evidence might include:
    *   Slang is used, e.g. "cheesed off".
    *   Humour is used, e.g. "River C and Swamp D".
    *   Contractions are used, e.g. "It's".

Answers

4. All your points should use relevant examples and terminology, and comment on the effects of the language used. Here are some things you could mention:
    *   Personification (the sun was "shining triumphantly"), suggesting that even inanimate objects reflect Konrad's positive attitude, creating an upbeat tone.
    *   A simile — the puddles "glittered like molten silver" — which takes something that is usually negative and presents it in a positive, beautiful way.
    *   The idea that everything "promised summer" and the phrase "for whom anything was possible," which create a sense of hope and optimism about the future.
5. All your points should use relevant examples and terminology, and comment on the effects of the language, tone and style used. Here are some things you could mention:
    *   An informal style that uses phrases like "up to your neck" and "bag loads of new skills", which encourage a young audience to connect with the writer.
    *   The inclusion of the sentence "There's nothing wrong with wanting a break." to show that the writer understands the mindset of young people.
    *   The short, punchy sentences that make up the last paragraph create a tone of excitement.
    *   Descriptive but simple adjectives ("incredible", "fantastic") to illustrate how fun the activities are.

Pages 28-29: Words and Phrases

1.

Adjectives	Adverbs
threatening	boastfully
lovely	tragically
phenomenal	bitterly
contemptuous	devotedly

2. E.g. "sneered" suggests that Angus doesn't really want to congratulate Madge.
3. E.g. "whispered" suggests that the speaker and listener are working together, whilst "spat" suggests that the speaker doesn't like the listener.
4. E.g. The phrase "I am sure" creates a confident tone that makes the reader more likely to agree with the author. The writer also refers to the reader as "my dear friend" to suggest familiarity, encouraging the reader to listen to the writer.
5. All your points should use relevant examples and terminology, and comment on the effects of the words and phrases used. Here are some things you could mention:
    *   The repetition of the word 'wind' — "a bitter wind, a stinging wind, a wind that drowned..." — to emphasise the overwhelming nature of the wind.
    *   Words and phrases that indicate noise: "roaring cacophony", "howling", "roar", to appeal to the reader's senses and make the storm more vivid.
    *   Violent verbs, such as "barged", "wrenched" and "savaged", to emphasise that the storm is destructive.
6. All your points should use relevant examples and terminology, and comment on the effects of the words and phrases used. Here are some things you could mention:
    *   Words and phrases associated with cold to emphasise the woman's detached personality ("icily", "stone cold").
    *   The phrases "breath caught painfully" and "sweat prickling like needles" suggest that the man's fear is physically painful.
    *   The simile "like a condemned man", which emphasises that the man feels resigned to his fate, and indicates that the woman is in a position of great power.

Pages 30-31: Metaphors, Similes and Analogy

1. a) M b) M c) S d) M
2. compares; images; non-fiction; persuade
3. E.g. The second text compares the water to something that the reader is familiar with, to make it easier to visualise.
4. E.g. The writer is trying to create the impression that the night sky is something precious and beautiful.
5. All your points should use relevant examples and terminology, and comment on the effects of the analogy used. Here are some things you could mention:
    *   The first paragraph establishes the idea of the sports car as something that you would "take pride in", which the writer can then refer back to throughout the text.
    *   The similarities between the Ferrari and the human body are emphasised, using mechanical terms like "fuel" and "systems" to refer to aspects of taking care of yourself. This persuades the reader that you should take as much care of the human body as you would a Ferrari.
    *   The writer emphasises the differences between a sports car and a human body to support their point further — they suggest that unlike a sports car, a human body is "priceless" and that you can't just "trade this engine in" for a new one, which persuades the reader that they should take even greater care of it.
6. All your points should use relevant examples and terminology, and comment on the effects of the metaphors and similes used. Here are some things you could mention:
    *   The use of a metaphor to make the environment seem hard and unforgiving — "The landscape was dull steel."
    *   The use of animal similes and metaphors to indicate how vulnerable the workers are — "like mice in a cage", "lambs" — in contrast to the soldiers, who are "wolves".
    *   The use of a simile to suggest the officer speaks in a forceful way — "fired his orders like cannon balls."

Pages 32-33: Personification, Alliteration and Onomatopoeia

1. a) personification. E.g. Makes the computer seem like it's mocking the writer, which conveys the writer's frustration.
   b) onomatopoeia. E.g. Helps the reader to imagine the noise created by the students.
   c) alliteration. E.g. Makes the text more memorable.
2. E.g.
    Personification: "a challenging foe"
    Effect of personification: makes the walk seem rewarding, by suggesting that the walkers have to fight something to complete it.
    Alliteration: "Wilderness Walk"
    Effect of alliteration: makes the name of the walk more memorable, so that readers remember to sign up for it.
3. All your points should use relevant examples and terminology, and comment on the effects of the onomatopoeia and personification used. Here are some things you could mention:
    *   The use of onomatopoeia such as "rustle", "cracking" and "shrill screech" to intrude upon the silence of the narrative and convey a sense of tension to the reader.
    *   Personification of the forest as a living being to create a sense of danger: "purposefully trying to deceive and confuse them."
    *   The personification of the shadows as "delighted", which contrasts with the generally menacing / unhappy tone of the extract, making the scene seem very sinister.

Answers

4. All your points should use relevant examples and terminology, and comment on the effects of the alliteration, onomatopoeia and personification used. Here are some things you could mention:
    *   Alliterative phrases such as "labyrinth of lost lanes" to emphasise how confusing the writer finds Kuala Lumpur.
    *   Personification of vehicles that "rumble past impatiently" which conveys the idea that everything in the city is animated and full of life.
    *   Onomatopoeic verbs such as "whine" and "buzz" help the reader to understand the writer's attitude to Kuala Lumpur as a loud and confusing place.

Pages 34-35: Irony and Sarcasm

1. opposite; intended; context; humour; offence; cruel
2. The second extract should be ticked.
    Examples should highlight the contradiction between the positive phrases, e.g. "Ivan is a brilliant secretary", and the negative context, e.g. "he keeps forgetting to bring a pen".
3. E.g. The writer uses irony to suggest that the characters have a light-hearted attitude to Maya's work. For example, Maya uses irony to joke about her job: "It's a trial, that's for sure."
4. All your points should use relevant examples and terminology, and comment on the effects of the irony and sarcasm used. Here are some things you could mention:
    *   The use of sarcasm to insult Brendan, indicating the writer's dissatisfaction with his service e.g. "highly skilled telephone operative".
    *   The writer's use of irony to express how much he dislikes the call centre process. He describes spending "twenty thrilling minutes" listening to hold music — his ironic tone shows his frustration at how long he had to wait.
    *   The use of irony in phrases like "slight hitch" and "lofty ambition" to add some humour to the text, which emphasises how ridiculous the writer finds the company.
5. All your points should use relevant examples and terminology, and comment on the effects of the irony and sarcasm used. Here are some things you could mention:
    *   The use of sarcasm in Hafsa's exchange with her father, ("we'll have a great time"), which suggests she's quite cheeky or disrespectful.
    *   The use of irony in Kirsty's narrative, "It really was going to be a fun-filled night", "it seemed like the fun never stopped". This conveys how much she dislikes schoolwork.
    *   The use of sarcasm when insulting Miss Hayward ("Very on trend.") to indicate that Hafsa can be cruel.

Pages 36-37: Rhetoric and Bias

1. a) hyperbole   b) parenthesis   c) antithesis
2. E.g. "Who has not felt outraged at the injustice of the world when viewing images of child poverty?"
    Technique: Rhetorical question
    Effect: It makes the reader think of child poverty as outrageous.
3. Evidence might include:
    *   gives the writer's opinion as fact ("By far the best hobby")
    *   makes generalisations, e.g. it claims that all young people "adore" playing cribbage
4. All your points should use relevant examples and terminology, and comment on the effects of the rhetorical devices used. Here are some things you could mention:
    *   Use of rhetorical questions such as "have you ever dreamt of... escaping on a luxury break?" to make the reader think about doing exactly that.
    *   Repeated use of lists of three, e.g. "lions, zebra and gazelle", to persuade the reader that there are many exciting options available to them.

*   The use of hyperbole to present a persuasive impression of the luxury nature of the holidays, such as "satisfy your every desire" and "your every wish will be catered for".
5. Answers should clearly compare the different ideas and techniques in each text, using quotations to support points. Here are some things you could mention:
    *   The writer of Source A has a fairly balanced viewpoint: they acknowledge positive aspects, like the room's size, as well as negative aspects, such as the "limited refreshment". This makes the writer seem more reasonable.
    *   The writer of Source B has a more negative viewpoint than the writer of Source A — they instantly "doubted" that the bedding was clean, which, combined with a complete absence of positive points about the room, shows that the writer is quite biased.
    *   Hyperbole is used in Source B to emphasise the writer's dislike of the hotel room — "hadn't been opened for about a century". The writer of Source A, however, uses discourse markers such as "Nevertheless" and "but" to show their more balanced viewpoint.

Pages 38-39: Descriptive Language

1. engaging; build; contrasting; agree
2. Descriptive adjectives: e.g. "blistering", "prickly"
    Describing different senses: e.g. "smelt of scorched grass", "feel the blistering sun"
    Descriptive verbs: e.g. "trudged", "shimmered"
    Imagery: e.g. "I felt as if I were underwater"
3. ii) Evidence might include:
    *   The use of a simile to make the noise easy to imagine.
    *   The onomatopoeic description of the "buzzing" stadium, which helps the reader to imagine the excitement.
4. All your points should use relevant examples and terminology, and comment on the effects of the descriptive language used, focusing on the contrasts between the two time periods. Here are some things you could mention:
    *   The use of descriptive language that appeals to the reader's sense of hearing, e.g. the "thundering noise" of the trains and the "clatter" of footsteps. This contrasts sharply with the "eerily quiet" station of the present day.
    *   The use of imagery in the phrase "like a visitor to a grave", which makes the station seem lifeless compared to how it was in the past, when it was "bustling".
    *   The first paragraph uses descriptive verbs such as "clung", "wandered" and "sag", which create an atmosphere of slowness and decay. In contrast, the second paragraph uses verbs that are associated with speed, e.g. "bustling", "skipped", "hurried".
5. Your answer should offer an opinion on the statement. It should comment on the techniques used to describe the party, using relevant examples and terminology to support each point. Here are some things you could mention:
    *   The cumulative effect of using several descriptive verbs together in "joking, laughing, making introductions", to convey a sense of action and excitement to the reader.
    *   Onomatopoeic verbs such as "thumping" and "clinking" to help the reader to imagine what the party sounds like.
    *   The focus on describing colours in the third paragraph, which appeals to senses to help the reader to visualise the upbeat mood of the party.

Pages 40-41: Narrative Viewpoint

1. perspective; third-person; detached; first-person; personal
2. a) third-person   d) second-person
    b) first-person   e) first-person
    c) third-person

Answers

3. Answers need to give an example from the text and explain why it's effective in the first person. E.g. The first-person narrator is effective in this extract because it allows an insight into the character's private emotions: the reader knows that she is feeling "terror" despite the fact that she has a "smile" on her face.
4. All your points should use relevant examples and terminology, and comment on the effects of the narrative viewpoint used. Here are some things you could mention:
   - Third person allows an insight into all of the characters' lives, which helps the reader to get to know their personalities. E.g. we know that the "young man" is nervous about his job interview as well as about the "exhaustion" of the "middle-aged woman".
   - Third person creates tension, because it can comment on the things that the characters aren't aware of: "a murder has been committed". This dramatic irony makes the reader care about the characters, as they have a sense of what's in store for them.
5. All your points should use relevant examples and terminology, and comment on the effects of the narrative viewpoint used. Here are some things you could mention:
   - The use of first person allows the reader access to Harry's thoughts, so they can get a better sense of his personality, e.g. "My heart was in my throat, I can tell you."
   - Harry's narrative uses colloquialisms, so the reader gets an insight into his background, e.g. "Buck up, Harry".
   - Harry's narrative viewpoint suggests that he's a humble man — he says "I'm not a hero." even though he describes his heroic actions.

Pages 42-43: Structure — Whole Texts
1. a) ii)   b) iv)   c) i)   d) iii)
2. a) description
   b) setting
   c) outside, inside
3. frame; story; move; multiple; characters
4. All your points should use relevant examples and terminology, and comment on the effects of the structural features used. Here are some things you could mention:
   - The shift in time that the extract uses — it starts in the present day, goes back to the past, then returns to the present. This allows the reader to become emotionally invested in Joan, so the ending has a greater impact.
   - The progression from "she had already been looking forward to the next visit", to "there wouldn't be a next visit", which emphasises the sadness of the fact that Joan's life is drawing to a close.
   - The motif of Joan looking at the sea, which is revisited in the first and last paragraph, and is contrasted by the way she "raced into the sea" in the second paragraph. This structure adds interest to the end of the story.
5. All your points should use relevant examples and terminology, and comment on the effects of the structural features used. Here are some things you could mention:
   - The first paragraph appeals to the senses to make the party seem exciting and active, e.g. "Pop music blared", "Rainbow-coloured balloons". The second paragraph doesn't use sensory descriptions, which makes the reader question the change in tone and focus on the boy.
   - The little boy is introduced at the end of the first paragraph, which acts as a cliffhanger, as the reader's focus is drawn to why he isn't part of the group of "screeching and laughing" children at the party.
   - The second cliffhanger, at the end of the extract, draws the reader's attention by leaving them wondering why the little boy is so unlike the other children in the story.

Pages 44-45: Sentence Forms
1. a) complex   d) complex
   b) compound   e) complex
   c) simple   f) compound
2. b) command. E.g. Commands create an authoritative tone, so a writer might use one to convince readers to take action.
   c) question. E.g. Questions make the reader think about their own response, so a writer might use one in order to get the reader on their side.
   d) exclamation. E.g. Exclamations are used to convey strong emotions, so a writer might choose this to help to persuade readers that they are passionate about what they're saying.
3. All your points should use relevant examples and terminology, and comment on the effects of the sentence forms used. Here are some things you could mention:
   - The long, complex sentence in paragraph one, which helps to build the reader's interest in the show.
   - The three consecutive short, simple sentences at the end of the second paragraph, which act as a cliffhanger to create a sense of Mikhail's panic and worry.
   - Sentences becoming generally shorter towards the end of the extract, to gradually increase the tension.
4. All your points should use relevant examples and terminology, and comment on the effects of the sentence forms used. Here are some things you could mention:
   - The use of a short sentence to begin the extract, which is dramatic and draws the reader in.
   - The very short sentences "Faster!" and "Still faster!" to increase the pace of the extract when Jane is about to win the race, which creates interest for the reader.
   - The long, complex sentence that begins "Thousands and thousands of people", which suggests that the response to Jane's triumph is overwhelming.

Section Four — Writing — Creative and Non-Fiction

Pages 46-47: Writing with Purpose
1.

Informative writing	Persuasive writing
an impersonal tone technical terms	rhetorical questions emotive language

2. Answers should include three separate points and a conclusion that summarises the argument, e.g.
   1) Gives a sense of identity within the school community.
   2) Means everyone looks the same, so they won't be bullied about their fashion choices.
   3) Counter argument: Uniform is expensive. However, works out cheaper — don't have to buy fashionable clothes.
   Conclusion: School uniform is cheaper, and makes for a more equal school community.
3. E.g. Hiding away in the sleepy village of Lyttlewich, Howtonshire, is a true gem of English architecture that you can't afford to miss. Thousands of visitors flock to the ancient Lyttlewich Church every year to marvel at its truly stunning artwork. Isn't it about time you joined the crowd?
4. Answers need to reflect purpose and audience using suitable vocabulary and language techniques. Answers should begin and end by directly addressing the audience, and be well-organised, clear and technically accurate. Here are some techniques you could include:
   - Rhetorical questions: "Do you really care about TV more than your health and wellbeing?"
   - Lists of three: "The more sleep you get, the happier, healthier and brainier you'll be."
   - Emotive language: "It's absolutely vital that you get enough sleep: your health and happiness depend on it."

Answers

5.   Answers need to reflect purpose and audience using suitable vocabulary and language techniques. Answers should begin and end by directly addressing the audience, and be well-organised, clear and technically accurate. Here are some techniques you could include:
- Facts and statistics: "Studies show that students involved in the arts are twice as likely to do well later in life."
- Repetition: "The arts help students to grow emotionally. The arts help students to communicate better. And above all, the arts help students to express their feelings."
- Clear point of view: "Creative subjects such as Art and Drama are incredibly important."

6.   Answers need to be entertaining for an audience of adult experts, using interesting language techniques to create a suitable tone and style. Writing needs to be structured and clear. Here are some techniques you could include:
- A dramatic opening: "Dwight's heart hammered as he pushed frantically against the pedals."
- Varied sentence structures: "Wham! The cyclist slammed into him, sending them both careering across the track."
- Descriptive words and phrases: "Dwight thrust his feet at the unforgiving ground, his pedals spiralling swiftly."

Pages 48-49: Writing for an Audience

1. b) E.g. The ear bones are some of the smallest in the body.
   c) E.g. Roman soldiers used weapons to defeat their enemies.
2. a) E.g. Money can be tricky to get your head around, so why aren't schools teaching us how to deal with it?
   b) E.g. Before you start making your yummy cake, ask an adult to help you get everything you'll need.
3.   E.g. I wish to complain about the quality of the fruit in the supermarkets of Townton. It is simply impossible to locate an unbruised apple, no matter how attentively one searches.
4.   Answers need to be entertaining for a friend your age. They need to use interesting language techniques to create a suitable tone and style. Writing needs to be structured and clear. Here are some techniques you could include:
- An interesting opening: "They were going to crash."
- Metaphor: "The waterfall was thunder; nothing else could be heard over its deafening roar."
- A cliffhanger ending: "They were safe for now, but there was a darker danger lurking just over the horizon."
5.   Answers need to reflect purpose and audience using suitable vocabulary and language techniques. Answers should begin and end by directly addressing the audience, and be well-organised, clear and technically accurate. Here are some techniques you could include:
- Alliteration: "Don't risk roaming the roads — stay safe on the pavement."
- A short sentence: "You face this danger every day."
- A memorable closing line: "Awareness of road safety can save lives — perhaps one day it will save yours."
6.   Answers need to be entertaining for an audience of adult regular readers. They need to use interesting language techniques to create a suitable tone and style. Writing needs to be structured and clear. Here are some techniques you could include:
- The five senses: "The air smelt of damp vegetation."
- Personification: "The leaves whispered in the night."
- A first-person narrator: "I shivered with cold as a brisk winter breeze crept into our tent."

Pages 50-51: Writing Stories

1.   engage; middle; character; direct; attention; clichés
2. a) E.g. First person, to give an insight into the character's thoughts and feelings.
   b) E.g. "Eerie", to make the forest seem scary and sinister. "Timid", to make the character seem afraid.

   c) E.g. "The moon was shining as brightly as a new penny."
3. a) E.g. I took a deep breath and stepped onto the alien spaceship, ready for my next adventure.
   b) E.g. The familiar sounds of the river rushing outside my window were all I needed to hear; I was finally home.
4.   Answers need to be entertaining for an audience of adults. They need to use interesting language techniques to create a suitable tone and style. Writing needs to be structured and clear. Here are some techniques you could include:
- Personification: "The flowers in the fields blinked shyly in the moon's light."
- An unusual character: "The town's oldest resident, Agatha Hart, was a tiny lady who wore layers of colourful, clashing clothing, which made her look at least twice her diminutive size."
- Direct address: "Perhaps you might think that nothing exciting could ever happen in a sleepy town like Drizzleford. You'd be wrong."
5.   Answers need to be entertaining for an audience of people your age, using interesting language techniques to create a suitable tone and style. Writing needs to be structured and clear. Here are some techniques you could include:
- A neat, satisfying ending: "The time had come; Jurgen returned the baby penguin to its mother, smiling wistfully at his memories of the fun they'd had."
- The five senses: "The smell of fish was overwhelming. Jurgen fought down the urge to gag as he inhaled the aromas of the penguin enclosure."
- Onomatopoeia: "The penguin's wings slapped excitedly."
6.   Answers need to be entertaining for an audience of travel experts, using interesting language techniques to create a suitable tone and style. Writing needs to be structured and clear. Here are some techniques you could include:
- An intriguing opening: "The train that carried Steve out of the city was exactly the same as the one he'd arrived on, after that fateful day all those years ago."
- Descriptive verbs: "The train slogged and toiled its way along the tracks."
- Personification: "The houses of the city seemed to watch him reproachfully as the train sped away."

Pages 52-53: Writing Descriptions

1. a) E.g. The tired car grumbled past unsteadily.
   b) E.g. The street lights were tree trunks in the jungle of the city.
   c) E.g. My face flushed as red as a tomato.
2. a) E.g. From the diving board, the swimmers below look like a shoal of brightly coloured fish.
   b) E.g. The noises in the pool echo like whalesong.
   c) E.g. I feel the roughness of the tiles under my bare feet.
   d) E.g. The bitter chlorine catches in the back of my throat.
3.   Answers should include ideas for descriptive techniques and devices that could be used to describe a family member.
4.   Answers need to entertain a reader your own age and explain why the building is interesting, using suitable tone, style and language techniques. Writing needs to be structured and clear. Here are some techniques you could include:
- Metaphor: "The seats are an ocean of blue fabric."
- The five senses: "You can hear your footsteps echo as you walk over the wooden boards."
- Onomatopoeia: "The curtains swish across the stage."
5.   Answers need to be entertaining for an adult. They need to use interesting language techniques to create a suitable tone and style. Writing should be structured and clear. Here are some techniques you could include:
- The five senses: "The sun felt warm on Gráinne's face."
- Metaphors: "The rock was a formidable enemy, and Gráinne had conquered it."
- Alliteration: "The solid slate sat sturdily under her shoes."

Answers

Pages 54-55: Writing Newspaper Articles

1. a) Purpose: to argue. Audience: pupils and teachers.
   b) E.g. Is our school not an ethnically diverse community?
   c) E.g. 38% of Wingwood's students are practising Christians.
   d) E.g. Frankly, this is hurtful discrimination.
2. E.g. Being rather financially stretched, I'm losing patience with these relentless requests to support endangered species.
3. b) E.g. Unlucky for you, kids — according to the government, it's 'no adult, no access'.
   c) E.g. Temperatures rocketed this weekend and, like a good Brit should, I immediately dug out our trusty barbecue.
4. Answers need to create an appropriate tone and style using suitable vocabulary and language techniques. Writing needs to be well-organised, clear and technically accurate. Answers should be clearly structured using features such as a headline, a strapline and subheadings. Here are some techniques you could include:
   - Hyperbole: "Classical music is humanity's greatest accomplishment; its loss would be incomprehensible."
   - Rhetorical questions: "How have we let it go this far? Other industries have adapted, why not us too?"
   - Lists of three: "How any listener can fail to be moved by Schubert's symphonies, Mahler's marches or Mozart's melodies is beyond me."
5. Answers need to create an appropriate tone and style using suitable vocabulary and language techniques. Writing needs to be well-organised, clear and technically accurate. Answers should be clearly structured using features such as a headline, a strapline and subheadings. Here are some techniques you could include:
   - Direct address: "You shouldn't spend too long staring at the screen of your tablet or smartphone."
   - Imperative verbs: "Start doing something active today."
   - Reassuring language: "It's okay if you haven't tried a sport before — most sports clubs welcome beginners."
6. Answers need to create an appropriate tone and style using suitable vocabulary and language techniques. Writing needs to be well-organised, clear and technically accurate. Answers should be clearly structured using features such as a headline, a strapline and subheadings. Here are some techniques you could include:
   - Metaphor: "For many, the looming spectre of endless debt is not an adequate deterrent."
   - Rhetorical questions: "What is so bad about this country? Why do millions of people spend so much hard-earned cash every year in trying to escape it?"
   - Quotes from experts: "'There are many exciting and unusual holidays to be had in the United Kingdom,' says top hotelier Lucy Meyers."

Pages 56-57: Writing Leaflets and Travel Writing

1. place; newspapers; opinions; entertain; conversational; first
2. a) Leaflet
   b) E.g. It uses layout features such as bullet points.
3. E.g. THE CHIPS ARE DOWN FOR FAST FOOD
   Do you care about the survival of the independent restaurants in our local area? If so, then you'll surely agree that it's time we banned fast-food chains for good.
4. Answers need to create an appropriate tone and style using suitable vocabulary and language techniques. Writing needs to be well-organised, clear and technically accurate. Answers should be clearly structured, using features such as a title, bullet points and subheadings. Here are some techniques you could include:
   - Direct address: "On Oakfall Island, there are dozens of different activities for you and your family to try."
   - Rhetorical questions: "Stuck for something to do this summer? Sick of visiting the same old places?"
   - Superlative adjectives: "It's simply the best holiday you'll ever have."
5. Answers need to create an appropriate tone and style using suitable vocabulary and language techniques. Writing needs to be well-organised, clear and technically accurate. Answers should be clearly structured, using features such as a title, bullet points and subheadings. Here are some techniques you could include:
   - Direct address: "You might get the chance to put your skills into practice on a school trip or exchange programme."
   - Imperative verbs: "Talk to teachers or older students to work out which language is right for you."
   - A friendly tone: "Languages can be tough at times, but there will be help and support available to you."
6. Answers need to create an appropriate tone and style using suitable vocabulary and language techniques. Writing needs to be well-organised, clear and technically accurate. Here are some techniques you could include:
   - Descriptive adjectives: "We should leap at the chance to swap humdrum, drizzly British life for something new."
   - First-person narrative: "In Bermuda, I saw a sunset so beautiful that it brought tears to my eyes."
   - Analogy: "Trying to understand different cultures without going out and experiencing them is a little like trying to paint a portrait of something without ever seeing it: basically, you're bound to get it wrong."

Pages 58-59: Writing Reports, Essays and Reviews

1. a) Report   b) Review
2. a) E.g. Whilst there are conflicting opinions on the issue, it seems clear on balance that we must scrap the tuition fee.
   b) E.g. The idea is completely inadvisable.
   c) E.g. My conclusion is that the council should invest its funds into a new community centre.
3. Answers should include an introduction, three clear points and a conclusion that summarises the argument, e.g.
   Introduction: Outlines main argument.
   1) Space programmes are a waste of money, which would be better spent on hospitals and schools.
   2) Counter argument: we can't live on Earth forever. But if we scrap space programmes, we can also invest in green energy so that we can live here longer.
   3) People have died exploring space (give examples).
   Conclusion: We should scrap most space exploration in order to invest in other, more important things.
4. Answers need to create an appropriate tone and style using suitable vocabulary and language techniques. Writing needs to be well-organised, clear and technically accurate. Here are some techniques you could include:
   - Clear, objective language: "The glottalbug is not an endangered species."
   - Facts and statistics: "Around 75% of our local agriculture relies on the glottalbug."
   - Linking phrases: "On the other hand, the glottalbug has caused significant environmental damage in other parts of the country."
5. Answers need to create an appropriate tone and style using suitable vocabulary and language techniques. Writing needs to be well-organised, clear and technically accurate. Here are some techniques you could include:
   - Counter arguments: "It has been argued that lowering the wages of footballers will result in an exodus of talent from the Premier League."
   - Facts and statistics: "The average wage of a top-flight footballer in the United Kingdom is almost 62 times that of the working population as a whole."
   - Balanced tone: "Whilst some footballers do donate to charity, it does not appear to be a widespread practice."

Answers

6.   Answers need to create an appropriate tone and style using suitable vocabulary and language techniques. Writing needs to be well-organised, clear and technically accurate. Here are some techniques you could include:
   *   First-person narrative: "I utterly adored this film."
   *   Hyperbole: "This film is a true giant in its genre; in thousands of years' time, we will still be talking about it."
   *   Analogy: "This film does for the romance genre what John Wayne did for the Western."

Page 60: Writing Speeches

1.   a) F   b) T   c) T
2.   b) E.g. What will we do when all the landfill sites are full?
   c) E.g. We must take better care of our planet!
   d) E.g. The landfill sites are heaving with decomposing food, unwanted packaging and broken appliances.
3.   Answers need to create an appropriate tone and style using suitable vocabulary and language techniques. Answers should begin and end by directly addressing the audience, and be well-organised, clear and technically accurate. Here are some techniques you could include:
   *   Direct address: "Fellow restaurant-owners, I'm appealing to you to make a decisive move."
   *   Repetition: "And whilst pizza is high in fat, high in calories and high in carbohydrates, it's also delicious."
   *   Rhetorical questions: "We all love pizza, don't we?"

Page 61: Writing Letters

1.

Purpose	To argue
Audience	Local council members
Register	Formal

2.   a) End: Yours sincerely
   b) Start: Dear Maria, End: E.g. Best wishes
   c) Start: Dear Sir / Madam, End: Yours faithfully
3.   E.g. "If year 11 students aren't provided with somewhere they can relax and study in peace, their stress levels will grow and their studying will become more difficult. Both of these things could result in a dip in grades across the board."
4.   Answers need to create an appropriate tone and style using suitable vocabulary and language techniques. Answers should be clearly structured using features such as the address of the sender and recipient; a greeting and sign-off; and the date. Writing needs to be well-organised, clear and technically accurate. Here are some techniques you could include:
   *   Formal language: "Dear madam, I write to express my concern over the state of the nation's housing supply."
   *   Anecdotal evidence: "I have witnessed dozens of young people struggle to find appropriate, affordable housing."
   *   Linking phrases: "Moreover, as a country, our population is crammed disproportionately into cities and towns."

Section Five — Sample Exams

Page 67: Paper 1, Question 1 — Sample Answers

2.   4 marks out of 4
   E.g. All four facts are true and can be found in lines 1 to 8 of the text.
3.   1 mark out of 4
   E.g. Fact A can be found in lines 1-8 and is true. However, fact C is false, and there is nothing about facts B or D in lines 1-8, so these don't get a mark.

Page 69: Paper 1, Question 2 — Sample Answers

1.   4 marks out of 8
   E.g. The answer uses some technical terminology and quotes, but not for every point it makes. It comments on some language effects, but it doesn't always explain how these link back to the question (e.g. the point about onomatopoeia).
2.   7 marks out of 8
   E.g. The answer makes a variety of detailed, sophisticated points, which are explained using good technical terminology and plenty of relevant quotes. The first paragraph could be better expressed, so the answer doesn't get full marks.

Page 71: Paper 1, Question 3 — Sample Answers

1.   8 marks out of 8
   E.g. The answer uses lots of sophisticated technical terminology (e.g. "imperative verb") and plenty of relevant examples to support its points. All of the points are explained clearly and in-detail, and a good range of structural features are discussed.
2.   2 marks out of 8
   E.g. The answer makes some simple comments about the text's structure, but it doesn't explain the effects of specific features, such as the "excited speech". Most quotes are relevant, but the last one isn't and there's hardly any technical terminology.

Page 73: Paper 1, Question 4 — Sample Answers

1.   11 marks out of 20
   E.g. The answer gives a range of examples in order to express a clear opinion on the statement. This is mostly explained clearly, using relevant quotations. The first paragraph explains the effect of the writer's choices well, but the second needs much more detailed analysis.
2.   8 marks out of 20
   E.g. The answer starts to give an opinion on the statement, and describes the effect of some of the writer's methods, such as the examples in the second paragraph. However, the examples about Doug stubbing his toe and not understanding the mother aren't clearly explained. Quotes are used to back up some points, but not all of them.

Page 75: Paper 1, Question 5 — Sample Answers

1.   Content and organisation = 11 marks out of 24
   Technical accuracy = 11 marks out of 16
   Total = 22 marks out of 40
   E.g. The content and organisation of the answer could do with some improvement — it attempts to use some structural features and language devices, but they're not always effective (e.g. "lit his face like a torch"), so the text isn't very engaging for its audience. The technical accuracy is better, but there's one spelling mistake and the answer could vary its punctuation and sentence forms more.
2.   Content and organisation = 23 marks out of 24
   Technical accuracy = 12 marks out of 16
   Total = 35 marks out of 40
   E.g. The content and organisation of the answer is imaginative and engaging. The second paragraph could be made slightly clearer. The technical accuracy of the answer is good, with a good range of vocabulary, but the punctuation could be more varied and interesting, and there is one punctuation error ("oak Street").

Page 81: Paper 2, Question 1 — Sample Answers

2.   3 marks out of 4
   E.g. Facts A, D and H are true, but fact C contradicts the text, so it doesn't get a mark.

Answers

3. 3 marks out of 4
E.g. Facts A, E and H are true, but fact G contradicts the text, so it doesn't get a mark.

Page 83: Paper 2, Question 2 — Sample Answers

1. 4 marks out of 8
E.g. Some differences between the two women are described, supported by some relevant quotations. However, the last paragraph needs more quotes to support its points, and it doesn't explain what Lesley's firing of Monica suggests about her opinions on childcare.
2. 8 marks out of 8
E.g. The differences between the two women are explained confidently and in depth, and perceptive inferences are made. The quotes fully support the points, and the points clearly contrast the two women.

Page 85: Paper 2, Question 3 — Sample Answers

1. 5 marks out of 12
E.g. There are some comments on the effects of language on the reader, although the analysis isn't very in-depth. Some technical terms are used, but "descriptive language" isn't used accurately. The answer uses some suitable quotes, but "can't help being shy" is irrelevant.
2. 11 marks out of 12
E.g. Appropriate quotations are used to illustrate interesting points, with technical terms used accurately throughout. Some points are expressed unclearly (e.g. "appeal to the relationship between") and the second paragraph is a bit repetitive, so the answer doesn't quite get full marks.

Page 87: Paper 2, Question 4 — Sample Answers

1. 6 marks out of 16
E.g. Some differences between the attitudes of the two writers are identified, supported by some relevant quotes. However, the quotes aren't analysed to explain the writers' methods, and "riotous" is inaccurate. The comparisons aren't always made clear, especially in the final sentence.
2. 16 marks out of 16
E.g. The answer makes interesting, detailed points about the writers' points of view, comparing them confidently and fully explaining the methods that each writer uses. It also supports each point with useful, precise evidence.

Page 89: Paper 2, Question 5 — Sample Answers

1. Content and organisation = 18 marks out of 24
Technical accuracy = 15 marks out of 16
Total = 33 marks out of 40
E.g. The answer is written clearly. It is generally well-suited to its form and purpose, but it uses some colloquial expressions (e.g. "In a nutshell") that are inappropriate for its audience. Technical accuracy is very good, but it could include a more interesting range of punctuation and sentence forms.
2. Content and organisation = 8 marks out of 24
Technical accuracy = 7 marks out of 16
Total = 15 marks out of 40
E.g. For the most part, this answer is too informal. It does use some structural techniques, but the structure would be improved by adding more paragraph breaks, and it needs more linguistic devices. The answer is mostly technically accurate, but there are a few mistakes, and it needs to use more sophisticated vocabulary and punctuation.

Section Six — Practice Exams

Pages 90-92: Paper 1

1. 1 mark for each valid response given, up to a maximum of four marks. Answers might include:
   - There are big bush-covered hills at the back
   - There are paddocks
   - There are bungalows
   - There's a sandy road
   - There are white dunes covered in reddish grass
   - There are fuchsias / nasturtiums / toi-toi grass
   - The bungalows have gardens with colourful plants

2. All your points should use relevant examples and terminology, and comment on the effects of the language used. Here are some things you could mention:
   - Descriptive verbs such as "huddled" are used to suggest that the sheep are fearful. This is reinforced by the words used to describe their movements: the sheep "trotted along quickly" as if in fear.
   - In contrast, the writer presents the dog as unafraid and even nonchalant. It runs along "carelessly" suggesting that it is "thinking of something else". This makes the roles of the animals clear: the dog is a working pet, whilst the sheep are animals in captivity.
   - The writer uses imagery to give really fine details of how the shepherd looks: his coat is "covered with a web of tiny drops". This detail helps to give the reader a clear picture of the shepherd, but also to help them feel the cold, wet conditions.
   - The entrance of the shepherd is described using a shorter, less detailed sentence than the ones that surround it ("And then in the rocky gateway the shepherd himself appeared."). This helps to make his entrance seem dramatic, which emphasises his character's importance.

3. All your points should use relevant examples and terminology, and comment on the effects of the structural features used. Here are some things you could mention:
   - The writer starts the text using short statements to give the reader the broadest facts about the scene, it is "Very early morning" and "The sun was not yet risen". This then progresses to much longer sentences to build the fine details of what the bay looks like. However, these are still broken up by a further short statement, "A heavy dew had fallen". In this way the writer manages to build detail, whilst emphasising the most important points so the reader feels how chilly, early and damp it is.
   - The focus then moves from the bay, "Round the corner" and begins to describe the animals and the shepherd. The descriptions given at this point are short, giving small insights: the sheep-dog is "old" and the shepherd is "a lean, upright old man". They act as introductions to the characters, drawing the reader further in to the scene.
   - In the long, final paragraph, the writer brings together the misty scene she has described with the characters she has introduced. The reader is taken on a short journey along the "sandy road" which continues to emphasise the "shadowy" early morning.
   - The paragraph ends with the revelation of the mist rapidly rolling away, revealing everything that was hidden in the first paragraph. This makes it feel to the reader as if the day has begun, and the opening of the story is now over.

Answers

4. Your answer should offer an opinion on the statement. It should comment on the techniques the writer uses to make the text detailed and interesting, using relevant examples and terminology to support each point.
    Here are some things you could mention:
    - I agree in some ways that it is like watching a film. Phrases such as "came into view" and "in the direction of the sea" create a cinematic effect for the reader, directing the reader's focus in the way that a camera might. In this section of the text it is effective as it allows the reader to see what the shepherd is seeing, drawing them into the scene with him.
    - However, the writer adds more detail than you would normally be able to experience in a film. She appeals to the senses as she describes the "whiff of eucalyptus" and the shepherd's "wet beard", which adds to the richness of the description and allows the reader to feel even more like they are inside the scene.

5. Answers to either question need to use an appropriate tone, style and register to match the purpose, form and audience. Writing needs to be well-organised, clear and technically accurate. Here are some techniques you could include:
    In a description:
    - Figurative language: "A faint curtain of mist rose off the lake, swathing everything in a sheet of fine white cloud."
    - Similes: "Just past the end of the jetty, waiting like a promise, was the little red boat."
    - Descriptive words and phrases: "Tendrils of gelatinous pond weed emerged from the water's edge."
    In the opening of a story:
    - An interesting, dramatic opening sentence: "The mist appeared too suddenly for them to avoid it."
    - An opening that directly addresses the reader: "If you'd seen what I saw on that misty October evening, you'd have done the same thing."
    - A descriptive opening that sets the scene: "The mist had emerged a few hours ago, curling slyly around the trunks of the gnarled old oaks in the wood."

Pages 93-96: Paper 2

1. 1 mark for shading each of the following statements:
    - A Jo is more hurt by Genevieve's lies than by her cancelling their plans.
    - C Jo relies on her long-term friendships.
    - E Jo is upset to see Genevieve when she arrives at the dinner party.
    - H Losing Genevieve as a friend is a significant moment in Jo's life.

2. Answers should use relevant quotes from both texts to summarise several differences between the two people. Here are some things you could mention:
    - Genevieve doesn't seem to care about her friend's feelings: she says she doesn't have to "explain herself" when she's hurt Jo. In contrast, the Boisterous Friend likes to check on his friend's wellbeing — he seems to have called round merely to check that Collins is "all right", and is simply "glad to have seen" him.
    - The Boisterous Friend is determined to see his friend (he "rushes in" to see Collins even when a servant seems to be trying to stop him), whilst Genevieve makes up excuses to avoid spending time with Jo.
    - The Boisterous Friend seems to be very fond of Collins. He uses terms of endearment such as "dear old boy" and "dear fellow". Genevieve, on the other hand, says her friendship with Jo has "run its course", which suggests she has no affection for her any more.

3. All your points should use relevant examples and terminology, and comment on the effects of the language used, focusing on how it is used to influence the beggar's listeners. Here are some things you could mention:
    - The beggar repeatedly uses the phrase "Good Christian people" to address the listeners directly, and engage them in his speech. This would have been a flattering address in the nineteenth century, which makes the listeners more likely to warm to the speaker.
    - The beggar uses a rhetorical question that contrasts his "starving" family with the "plenty" that others have, to make the listeners reflect on their own wealth and pity his poverty.
    - Verbs such as "injured" and "deprived" would make listeners empathise with the injustice the beggar suffers, which might persuade them to help him.

4. Answers should clearly compare the different attitudes and techniques in each text, using quotations to support points. Here are some things you could mention:
    - Collins seems to find friendship tiresome: the way he lists the friends he could "dispense" with in the penultimate paragraph emphasises his determined attitude towards parting with all of them. Russell, in contrast, believes that there are "powerful reasons" for maintaining friendships. The word "bonds" suggests that she feels friendships are strong ties that should not be broken.
    - The repeated use of the phrase "I could dispense" shows Collins' confidence in his attitude to friendship. On the other hand, Russell's questions about whether people fit into the "first dozen" or the "remotest 90" of their friends' circles demonstrate her belief that people in modern society need reassurance about the exact state of their friendships.
    - Collins may well be writing satirically. His terms of familiarity, such as "dear", hint at a true fondness for his friends, and his complaint that one friend "never does really" ask him to dinner could imply that he does want to socialise after all. Jenni Russell, in contrast, writes with an earnest tone to offer a genuine answer to her title question: "What are friends for?" Readers might be amused by Collins' article, whilst Russell seems to be aiming to share her thoughts and potentially inspire readers to work hard at their friendships.

5. Answers need to use an appropriate tone, style and register to match the purpose, form and audience. Writing needs to be well-organised, clear and technically accurate. Answers should be clearly structured using features such as a headline, a strapline and subheadings. Here are some techniques you could include:
    - Direct address: "If you're like me, social media sites have become a vital means of communicating with real-life friends who you can no longer meet face-to-face."
    - Antithesis: "Face-to-face friendships are certainly real, but not all real friendships are face-to-face."
    - Satirical language: "People who worry about the influence of social media are probably the same people who believe that deadly, invisible toxins emanate from the speaker of every mobile phone."